Da.. Ka..

D0851719

'NG CO.
1L LIBRARY
.67-1612

E-BOAT
vs
MTB

The English Channel 1941–45

GORDON WILLIAMSON

First published in Great Britain in 2011 by Osprey Publishing,
Midland House, West Way, Botley, Oxford, OX2 0PH, UK
44-02 23rd Street, Suite 219, Long Island City, NY 11101, USA
E-mail: info@ospreypublishing.com

© 2011 Osprey Publishing Ltd.

All rights reserved. Apart from any fair dealing for the purpose of private study,
research, criticism or review, as permitted under the Copyright, Designs and Patents
Act, 1988, no part of this publication may be reproduced, stored in a retrieval
system, or transmitted in any form or by any means, electronic, electrical, chemical,
mechanical, optical, photocopying, recording or otherwise, without the prior
written permission of the copyright owner. Enquiries should be addressed to the
Publishers.

A CIP catalogue record for this book is available from the British Library

Print ISBN: 978 1 84908 406 2
PDF e-book ISBN: 978 1 84908 407 9

Gordon Williamson has asserted his right under the Copyright, Designs and Patents
Act, 1988, to be identified as the Author of this Work.

Page layout by: Ken Vail Graphic Design, Cambridge, UK
Index by Alan Thatcher
Typeset in ITC Conduit and Adobe Garamond
Maps by bounford.com
Originated by PDQ Digital Media Solutions, Suffolk, UK
Printed in China through Bookbuilders

11 12 13 14 15   10 9 8 7 6 5 4 3 2 1

Osprey Publishing is supporting the Woodland Trust, the UK's leading woodland
conservation charity, by funding the dedication of trees.

www.ospreypublishing.com

CONTENTS

INTRODUCTION

The Battle of the Atlantic, and the war waged between Hitler's U-Boats and Allied escort forces, have understandably been the focus of much attention in the years since the end of World War II. Yet a smaller, but equally important, battle raged much closer to Britain's shores, as German and British coastal forces struggled for supremacy in the waters of the English Channel and southern North Sea, each striving to interdict the other's vital supply convoys.

The powerful German E-Boats – fast, well-armed torpedo boats – wrought such damage amongst Allied shipping that the approaches to the English Channel, and especially the area between The Wash and Great Yarmouth, became known as 'E-Boat Alley'. With a maximum of three convoys per week, each of up to 50 ships, sailing along the east coast of Britain, targets for the Germans were plentiful.

Britain began the war with woefully weak Coastal Forces to combat the E-Boat threat. By the end of the war, however, the situation had been reversed, with the battered and shrunken Schnellbootwaffe (S-Bootwaffe – 'Fast Boat Arm') hugely outnumbered by the British and with the RAF having complete control of the skies over the contested waters. Nevertheless, the E-Boats had come second only to the U-Boats in the enemy tonnage they had sunk.

In boat design too, the British entered the war at a disadvantage with a disparate range of boat types, none of which in their own right was a match for even the early E-Boat types. The potent torpedo-armed Motor Gun Boats (MGBs) that the Royal Navy could boast by 1945, however, were perfectly capable of besting the bigger E-Boats and often did.

OPPOSITE
This photo, taken from the E-Boat immediately ahead of the one in the shot, shows how high the bow of the boat was raised when travelling at speed, though in fact this effect was far less pronounced on German boats than on their British equivalents. (Author's collection)

CHRONOLOGY

1930
7 July   The first of the Kriegsmarine's E-Boats, S 1, is launched by the Lürssen yard in Bremen-Vegesack.

1935
Founding of the first of Germany's full-strength E-Boat flotillas with the expansion of 1. Schnellbootshalbflottille into 1. Schnellbootsflottille, based in Kiel under Korvettenkapitän Hans Dietrich Conrady.

1937
March   The first British torpedo-boat flotilla, 1 MTB Flotilla, formed under the command of Lt Cdr Guy B. Sayer.

May   Initially a private venture, the Vosper company's new torpedo boat design is accepted into the Royal Navy as MTB 102.

1940
16 May   Oberleutnant Hermann Opdenhoff, commander of S 31, becomes the first E-Boat commander to be decorated with the Knight's Cross of the Iron Cross.

31 October   Rear Admiral P.K. Kekewich appointed as commander of RN Coastal Forces.

1941
17 April   First major engagement between E-Boats and British MTBs takes place during a German attack on convoy FS64 near Great Yarmouth.

19/20 November   MGBs of 6 MGB Flotilla attack five E-Boats off the Hook of Holland. One becomes the first E-Boat to be boarded by enemy forces, but sinks shortly afterwards.

1942
11 February   E-Boats and MTBs clash during British attempts to intercept the German warships *Scharnhorst*, *Gneisenau* and *Prinz Eugen* during the so-called 'Channel Dash'.

20 April   Post of Führer der Schnellboote created under Kapitän zur See und Kommodore Rudolf Petersen. Command of the E-Boats had previously sat with the Führer der Torpedoboote.

21/22 April   MGBs from 6 MGB Flotilla under the command of Lt Cdr Robert P. Hichens attack and drive off a superior force of E-Boats in the waters off Ostend.

22 September   Lt Cdr Hichens is awarded the DSO and Bar by King George VI for his attack on E-Boats during April.

13 November   Kapitänleutnant Werner Töniges, commander of S 102, becomes the first recipient of the rare E-Boat War Badge with Diamonds following the award of the Oakleaves to his Knight's Cross of the Iron Cross.

1943
18 February   A major E-Boat operation is foiled by an ambush from a force of British destroyers and MGBs supported by Fairey Albacore aircraft. S 71 is sunk.

MTB 218 at speed during her trials. Originally ordered on a private contract for the Greek Navy, she was subsequently requisitioned for the Royal Navy. (BAE Systems Surface Ships South, late Vosper Thornycroft Shipbuilding)

24 October A failed attack on Convoy FN1160 sees the German forces driven off with the loss of S 88.

1 November The last of Germany's E-Boat flotillas, 24. Schnellbootsflottille, is created from former Italian vessels seized after the Italian surrender.

1944

27 April Disaster at Slapton Sands when landing craft involved in Exercise *Tiger*, the practice landing for the D-Day invasion, is attacked by E-Boats and large losses incurred.

12 June Three British transport ships delivering munitions to the Allied bridgehead in Normandy sunk by S 177 and S 178.

14 June Severe damage to the E-Boat bunkers in Le Havre caused by major British bombing raid.

18 August E-Boats from 8. S-Bootsflottille successfully protect a breakout by over 100 vessels from the encircled port of Le Havre despite attacks from MTBs and destroyers.

1945

19/20 March Mines laid by E-Boats result in the sinking of two British transports, a Landing Ship, Tank and an American Liberty Ship.

12/13 April Final action of the war between E-Boats and MTBs in British coastal waters.

The highly polished ventilators on this MTB motoring along at low speed are a clue to the fact that this boat, produced in 1940, was not for Royal Navy use, but one of just three sold to Romania, then neutral. The diminutive size of these craft is apparent from this shot. (BAE Systems Surface Ships South, late Vosper Thornycroft Shipbuilding)

DESIGN AND DEVELOPMENT

THE GERMAN E-BOATS

In the area of fast, light motor boats, the Germans spent most of their effort in developing and improving one particular type, the *Schnellboot* (literally 'Fast Boat') or S-Boat. (Note: The term E-Boat is generally accepted to have been a British term derived from the designation 'Enemy Boat'. This term is far more widely recognized than the correct term S-Boat.) In reality, when considering this type of craft, and especially when comparing it to equivalent British vessels, consideration should also be given to the *Räumboot* or R-Boat, a small motor-minesweeper. Between them the S-Boats and R-Boats covered many of the same tasks handled by the greater variety of British small motor boats.

Germany had a long history of involvement in the construction of high-quality and extremely fast motor boats. In particular, the well-known firm of Otto Lürssen had, in 1908, already produced a small motor boat capable of speeds of up to 50 knots. Lürssen continued to produce motor boats for the Kaiserliche Marine in World War I, and also after the war when the new Weimar Republic sought to rebuild the German Navy, now known at the Reichsmarine, from the decimated remains of the Kaiser's fleet. Allied prohibitions on the number of large ships Germany was permitted to own and build meant that small warships would take on a greater importance.

Though Germany possessed a small fleet of torpedo boats, these were not the fast attack craft like the later Anglo-American-style Motor Torpedo Boats (MTBs), but larger, much slower, steam-driven boats. Displacing around 900 tonnes, they were almost the size of a small destroyer. Yet boats developed under the guise of civilian speedboats were used in the mid-1920s, albeit unarmed, on secret training exercises with larger surface warships to prove the concept of the fast, manoeuvrable, torpedo-carrying boat. Once again the Lürssen firm was heavily involved, as were others such as Abeking & Rasmussen in Bremen and the Kaspar-Werft in Travemünde. The intended use of these craft was hidden behind the designation 'UZ(s) U-Boot Zerstörer (schnell)' or 'Fast U-Boat Destroyer'.

There were three main methods of delivering the boat's payload – the torpedo:

Stern launch – tail first. This rather dangerous-sounding method saw torpedoes being launched tail first (i.e. nose pointing in the same direction as the boat) from tubes at the stern, which then required the boat to make a tight turn to port or starboard to avoid its own torpedoes.

Stern launch – nose first. This required the boat to turn 180 degrees away from the target and launch torpedoes towards the enemy whilst it made off in the opposite direction. This method had some merit and was actually used on some very small E-Boats.

Bow launch. The bow launch was to become the standard method, with torpedo tubes mounted on the bow of the boat, launching the torpedo nose first towards the target. The same method was eventually adopted by most other countries, including Great Britain and the United States.

In 1930, the Lürssen firm once again became involved in the manufacture of motor torpedo boats for the navy on an official basis. The first modern E-Boats would be the 52-tonne UZ(s) 16 (eventually to be renumbered as S 1). The new boat designs soon proved themselves, and formed the basis for all future E-Boat development.

It was normal for torpedo boats to fire both port and starboard tubes at the same time, as the pressure from firing a torpedo from just one side would skew the fast-moving boat off course. (BAE Systems Surface Ships South, late Vosper Thornycroft Shipbuilding)

THE BRITISH MOTOR BOATS

The British Coastal Forces had access to a far greater range of small motor boats than did their German counterparts. For the purposes of this work, there are four main types to consider.

MOTOR TORPEDO BOAT (MTB)

The two principal types of MTB produced for the Royal Navy were both manufactured by Vosper. Founded in the late 18th century, Vosper had originally been an engineering firm that moved into the production of maritime engines, before becoming involved in the construction of small boats during World War I.

In the mid-1930s, Vosper began to design its own fast powerboats, aiming to secure contracts for the manufacture of such vessels for the Royal Navy. Its first boat was constructed as a private venture, but was accepted by the Navy in 1937, when it became MTB 102.

The first major type, produced from 1940, was the Vosper 70ft MTB. The type displaced 55 tonnes. The first ten were powered by three 900hp Hall-Scott Defender engines, and the remainder by three Packard 4M-2500 marine engines, giving a top speed of around 39 knots. As well as the main engines, two Ford V8 auxiliary engines were carried. The 70ft MTB carried two 21in torpedo tubes as well as, typically, two .5in and up to four .303in machine guns, with the option to fit four Mk VII depth charges.

From 1943, Vosper began production of the 73ft MTB. Displacing 47 tonnes, these were also powered by three Packard marine engines and could attain a top speed of 40 knots. This larger type carried four 18in torpedo tubes as well as a twin 20mm Oerlikon cannon, two twin Vickers .303in machine guns mounted on each of the aft torpedo tubes and a single .5in machine gun mounted on each of the forward tubes. A second type was later produced with only two torpedo tubes, but a heavier gun armament consisting of a 6pdr gun on the fore deck, as well as a 20mm Oerlikon cannon at the stern and Vickers .303in machine guns.

MTBs, fast and well armed, were ideal weapons with which to attack slow-moving enemy merchant ships but, being smaller, of less robust construction and generally carrying lighter armament than their German opposite numbers, were at a great disadvantage should they encounter the heavier, tougher enemy E-Boats.

A nice clear view of the fore deck of an early boat, MTB 36, shows a very uncluttered space. Note the two anti-slip walkways. With only very modest armament, these boats depended on their speed to strike and make their getaway as quickly as possible. (BAE Systems Surface Ships South, late Vosper Thornycroft Shipbuilding)

VOSPER TYPE I MTB

The Vosper firm was responsible for many of the major MTB types used by the Royal Navy in World War II. Illustrated here is the 73ft Vosper Type I. Powered by three Packard engines developing a total of 4,200bhp, this type was capable of top speeds of around 40 knots. Displacement was around 47 tonnes (around half the displacement of most E-Boat types) and a crew of 13 was carried. This type carried four 18in torpedo tubes. A 20mm Oerlikon cannon was carried on a platform in front of the bridge and additional armament could consist of two twin Vickers K .303in machine guns on pintle mounts on the aft torpedo tubes and two single-barrel Browning .30cal machine guns on pintle mounts on the forward torpedo tubes. Typical colour schemes for this type included two-tone grey hulls with dark grey horizontal surfaces (decks) and paler grey superstructure. The pennant number was usually carried in black on the hull side. This type entered service in 1944 and was also used for delivering and recovering agents from occupied France. Around 76 of them were lost to enemy action during World War II.

19ft 4in

73ft

19ft 4in

MOTOR GUN BOAT (MGB)

The most important of the gun boat types built for the Royal Navy were produced by Fairmile Marine. Three main types were designed, lettered B through to D. Only small numbers (24) of the C type were made, so for the purposes of this work we will concentrate on the types built in greatest numbers.

The Fairmile B

The Fairmile B was a relatively large vessel at 34m and, with a displacement of 85 tonnes, was much larger than any MTB. It was powered by two Hall-Scott Defender petrol engines, which developed 650bhp each, giving it a top speed of 20 knots. Typical armament was one 3pdr gun on the fore deck, a twin .303in machine gun mount and 12 depth charges. Well over 600 of the type were built, and with armour protection for the bridge, these larger boats were far better placed to withstand combat with E-Boats than the lighter, unarmoured MTBs.

The Fairmile D

The Fairmile D was slightly larger than its predecessor at 35m and slightly heavier at 90 tonnes. It was powered by four Packard 2500 petrol engines, each developing 1,250bhp and giving the boat a useful top speed of 29 knots. Just under 230 of the type were built, from 1942 onwards.

The Fairmile D was a highly versatile design and could be built in at least three basic versions: the standard MGB configuration; the MTB configuration, created by adding torpedo tubes; and also as an Air-Sea Rescue Launch (ASRL). In MGB

Looking towards the bridge and wheelhouse of a 70ft Vosper Type I MTB. Note the large spray deflectors around the edge of the bridge and the Plexiglas windscreen, both essential features given the amount of spray these boats encountered when travelling at speed. (BAE Systems Surface Ships South, late Vosper Thornycroft Shipbuilding)

The bridge area on a 70ft Vosper Type I is shown here to good effect. Note the compass housing in front of the steering wheel and the throttle levers just to its left. (BAE Systems Surface Ships South, late Vosper Thornycroft Shipbuilding)

configuration, the boat would carry a typical armament of one 2pdr gun, one twin 20mm Oerlikon, two .5in machine guns and four Vickers .303in machine guns.

MOTOR LAUNCH (ML)

Fairmile Marine was also responsible for the production of a motor launch, the Fairmile A. This vessel was 33.5m in length and displaced some 57 tonnes. Powered by three Hall-Scott Defender V12 petrol engines developing 600bhp each, it had a top speed of 25 knots. It was armed with a 3pdr gun forward, two .303in Lewis guns and the capacity to carry up to 12 depth charges. Only 12 of this type were built, however. The launch type built in greatest numbers was the so-called HDML or Harbour Defence Motor Launch, of which nearly 500 were produced.

AIR-SEA RESCUE LAUNCH (ASRL)

The best known of the ASRLs was the so-called 'whaleback' design produced by the British Powerboat Company. Some 19.2m in length and displacing 21.5 tonnes, it could achieve a top speed of around 36 knots powered by three Napier Sea Lion engines. It was relatively well armed with two glazed turrets very similar to those carried on aircraft, each with a .303in machine gun. Either side of the bridge were mounted twin .303in machine guns with armoured shields and facing aft on the rear deck was a 2cm Oerlikon cannon. A total of 69 of the type were built between 1940 and 1942, and remained in service in the waters of the English Channel until 1945, saving the lives of many Allied aircrew.

Unlike larger warships, the small boats were not built in shipyards as such, but in smaller boat sheds as seen here. This policy meant that the builders were able to work in relative comfort in all weathers. (BAE Systems Surface Ships South, late Vosper Thornycroft Shipbuilding).

A huge contribution to the coastal battles against the Kriegsmarine was made by boats with a non-torpedo primary armament. In fact, as the number of targets suitable for torpedo attack declined, many craft intended as MTBs were either completed as, or converted to, MGBs. (Note that these craft are not drawn to the same scale.)

Motor Gun Boat (a)
Built to counter the E-Boat menace in the Channel, MGBs carried a powerful armament for their relatively small size. Here we see MGB 75, built by the British Powerboat Company. At a shade under 72ft in length, this vessel displaced 34 tonnes and had a top speed of 43 knots. She carries a 2pdr gun forward and a 20mm Oerlikon aft, as well as two twin .303in Vickers K machine guns aft. Some MGBs had even heavier armament, as well as carrying depth charges.

Fairmile B Motor Launch (b)
This was an extremely versatile craft that could be put to use in several roles: it could be used as a rescue launch or have torpedo tubes added to become an MTB, and was often used as a submarine chaser. At 112ft long, the type displaced 85 tonnes and was powered by two Hall-Scott Defender petrol engines, developing a total of 1,300bhp and giving a top speed of 20 knots. This example has a Browning machine gun forward; typical armament would include a 3pdr gun and a twin .303in Vickers K machine-gun mount as well as a complement of depth charges.

Air-Sea Rescue Launch (c)
This distinctive type of launch with its 'whaleback' lines was manufactured by the British Powerboat Company. It was 63ft in length and displaced 21.5 tonnes. Its Napier Sea Lion 500bhp engines gave it a top speed of 36 knots. Armament consisted of two Armstrong-Whitworth turrets similar to those carried in aircraft, each with a .303in Vickers K machine gun, and a 20mm Oerlikon cannon at the stern. The typical colour scheme consisted of a black hull and dark grey superstructure. The pennant number was carried at the bow, along with an RAF roundel.

OTHER BRITISH COASTAL CRAFT

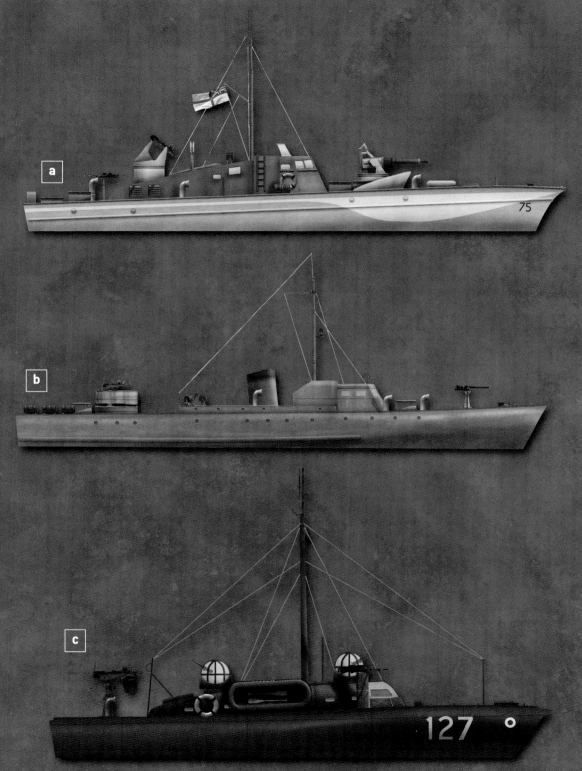

TECHNICAL SPECIFICATIONS

THE E-BOAT

The E-Boat underwent continuous improvement and development over the 15-year period from the launch of the first of the type until the end of World War II. Around 13 identifiable types were produced, many of the differences relating to engine types, speed, etc., with several sub-types being visually identical or at least very similar to one another. For the purposes of this work, there are really three main types to consider.

EARLY LOW FORECASTLE TYPES

S 1–S 25

The first six boats to be built, S 1–S 6, were all constructed by Lürssen. They had displacements ranging from 58 to 85 tonnes and were 27–33m in length. The E-Boat design at this time was still very much a work in progress, and various powerplants were tried, not always with great success. The overall concept was workable, however, and although all of the first six boats were ultimately sold to Spain, by the time Lürssen began work on the next batch (S 7–S 13) a basically sound format had been achieved. These boats had a length of 32.4m, a beam of 5.1m and they displaced 86 tonnes. Three of these boats (S 7–S 9) were fitted out with MAN diesels and others (S 10–S 13) with the more reliable Daimler-Benz type.

S 14–S 17 were slightly larger again. Displacing 93–100 tonnes, these vessels were 34.6m in length with a beam of 5.3m. A crew of 18 was required. These four boats were powered by MAN 11-cylinder two-stroke diesels, which proved so unreliable that it was decided not to use this firm's engines in future E-Boats. The last eight boats of this early type (S 18–S 25) were of very similar specification and identical in size to the S 14 class, but were powered by the Daimler-Benz MB 501 four-stroke diesel, a far more reliable unit.

All of these early boats had a low forecastle, usually with a single machine-gun mount on the fore deck between the torpedo tubes. Four torpedoes were carried and a 2cm Flak gun mounted amidships provided limited anti-aircraft protection.

MID-WAR HIGH FORECASTLE TYPES

S 26 class (S 26–29, 38–53, 62–133, 159–166)

The S 26 models were also built by Lürssen and had the forecastle raised, so that it enclosed the torpedo tubes. Displacing 112 tonnes, they were 34.9m in length with a beam of 5.3m. These boats required a crew of 24. Like the earlier boats, they were powered by the 20-cylinder Daimler-Benz MB 501.

S 30 class (S 30–37, 54–61)

Also built by Lürssen, the S 30 class was marginally smaller than the S 26, displacing 100 tonnes and having a length of 32.8m and beam of 5.1m. The slightly smaller size was due to the fitting of the 16-cylinder Daimler-Benz MB 502 engine. This class also required a crew of 24.

LATE-WAR ARMOURED BRIDGE TYPES

S 139 class (S 139–150, 167–169, 171–227, 229–260)

This class was visually quite similar to the S 26 type, but was in fact 1m greater in length and was powered by the supercharged Daimler-Benz MB 511 engine. Each of this type had a much lower profile due to the new, armoured bridge design. Armoured bridges were in fact also fitted from S 67 onwards in the S 26 class, but were common to all the S 139 and S 170 classes.

A flotilla of E-Boats at sea. These are later boats with the raised forecastle, enclosed torpedo tubes and armoured bridge. The barrel of the 2cm cannon, in its tub near the bow, is just visible. (Author's collection)

LOW FORECASTLE E-BOAT: S 7

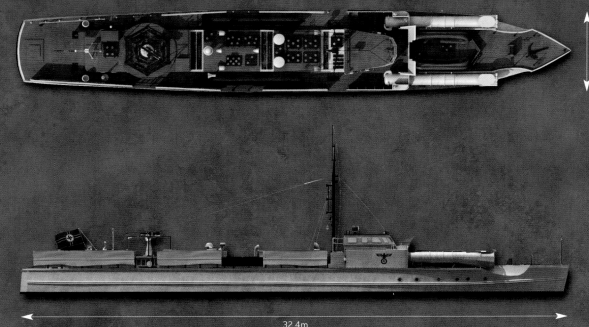

4.9m

32.4m

There were several early E-Boat types that were made in limited numbers only. Shown here is the S 7 type of which just seven examples were made during 1932 by the Lürssen firm in Bremen. Deck armament consisted of a single 2cm Flak gun mounted on a platform towards the stern. A single machine gun could also be mounted on a pedestal between the torpedo tubes on the foredeck. She carries the typical E-Boat colour scheme of very pale grey, a shade officially known as *Schnellbootsweiss*. The torpedo tubes are mounted externally on the forward deck with just two G7 torpedoes being carried. Capable of speeds of up to 35–36 knots, the first three built were powered by MAN diesels and the remainder with Daimler-Benz diesels, final decisions on the type of engines to be used not yet having been made. Displacing around 90 tonnes and 32.4m in length, they carried a crew of up to 23. Their limited armament led to these early boats being deployed onto less testing duties on the outbreak of war, such as training and general patrol duties or sub-chasing work. Interestingly, all of them survived the war.

4.9m

S 170 class (S 170–228, 301–425, 701–825)

The S 170 class was to be the largest of the E-Boats. Displacing 121 tonnes, they were 35m in length and had a beam of 5.3m. The last batch to be constructed, S 701–S 825, was also powered by the supercharged MB 511 engine. These later E-Boats were much more heavily armed than those with which the Kriegsmarine began the war. Typically, a 2cm gun was fitted in a sunken 'tub' on the forecastle, with twin 2cm guns amidships and either a 3.7cm gun or a quadruple 2cm mount (the so-called *Flakvierling*) towards the stern. These boats also regularly carried mines or depth charges.

THE R-BOAT

In addition to E-Boats, the Germans made much use of the R-Boats on the Channel coast. These were (relatively) fast motor launches that could fulfil a number of tasks, including convoy escort, sub-chasing, minelaying, minesweeping and air-sea rescue work.

The appearance of the R-Boat was quite similar to the E-Boat, with the most obvious difference being the lack of torpedo tubes. The very first types made pre-war were 26m in length and displaced only about 60 tonnes, but by 1939 they had grown to around 38m in length and displaced 125 tonnes. Some, like the R 301 type, reached 41m in length with a 160-tonne displacement. Top speed was somewhat slower than for the E-Boats, typically around 20 knots, but they could carry a fairly heavy armament with two 2cm and one 3.7cm guns backed up with machine guns, and carrying a payload of mines and/or depth charges. Some of the R 301 type even ended up having torpedo tubes fitted, though this was a rare event for R-Boats.

One very special aspect of *some* of these boats was the fitting of Voith-Schneider cycloidal drive propellers, which allowed a phenomenal degree of manoeuvrability, enabling the vessel to change direction almost instantly. Around 300 R-Boats were built, with somewhere in the region of 50 per cent of their number being lost to enemy action.

A typical *Räumboot*, or R-Boat, a motor-minesweeper often called upon to perform similar duties to the E-Boats, particularly with respect to protecting coastal convoys. (Author's collection)

LAYOUT AND CONSTRUCTION

The E-Boats' hulls were of mixed wooden/metal construction, with the keel, longitudinals and deck beams in wood and the frames and diagonal stringers in light metal alloy. Deck superstructures were also in light metal alloys. The bulkheads were in 4mm-thick steel below the waterline and in slightly thinner, light metal alloy above the waterline.

Inside the hull, the forwardmost compartment contained the WCs and washroom for the crew. Moving through the first bulkhead, the next area contained the petty officers' accommodation, with bunks for five men, plus a small compartment for the coxswain. Through the next bulkhead was, on the port side, the radio room, and on the starboard, the captain's cabin. Moving aft, the following compartment contained two large fuel cells, one either side of the central walkway. These contained up to 6,000 litres of fuel.

In these mid-engined boats, the central compartment contained the two diesel engines that powered the outer port and starboard shafts, with a walkway between them. The next compartment housed the centrally mounted diesel engine that drove the middle shaft, with walkways either side. The subsequent compartment contained yet more fuel cells, capable of holding almost 8,000 litres of diesel fuel.

A senior NCO and junior rating in the cramped engine room of an E-Boat. Note that life jackets are worn, even in the interior of the boat. (Hermann Büchting via R. Mills)

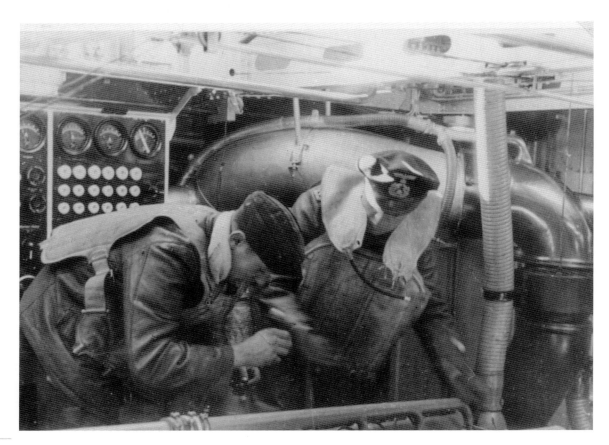

The penultimate compartment was the lower ranks' accommodation area, which normally housed up to 15 men as well as the boat's magazine. Finally, the small aftermost compartment housed yet more fuel cells, typically holding up to 4,000 litres.

ARMAMENT

Machine guns

The basic machine gun armament aboard E-Boats was the 7.92mm MG38 or the MG42, which had the facility to be belt- or magazine-fed, though earlier MG08 and MG151 types were also widely used. The MG38 and MG42 were excellent weapons, and were the main general-purpose machine guns of the German Army. Both had an effective range of up to around 2,000m, with a cyclic rate of 900rpm for the MG38 and up to 1,550rpm for the MG42. The high rates of fire made these weapons quite devastating. The downside, however, as already discovered by the army, was that the guns required substantial supplies of ammunition. This could be problematic for infantry or other troops having to carry heavy ammunition containers in the field, but onboard ship it was less of a problem. A number of dismounted machine guns were also carried, which could be fitted to various mounts when necessary.

This E-Boat has the heavier 4cm Bofors cannon as its aft armament, capable of delivering a nasty shock to any British boat attempting to approach or pursue the German craft from astern. (Hermann Büchting via R. Mills)

On many of the later boats, the forward machine gun was replaced by a heavier 2cm MG C/38 cannon, giving the boat much more 'punch' when firing forward. In many cases, however, the option to fire forward would be limited, as when travelling at speed the bow would rise in the water quite significantly, obscuring the gunner's view of the seas in front of him.

Flak guns

Early boats carried a 2cm MG C/30 Flak gun on a pedestal mount sited on a circular platform amidships, over the engine room. This was the same weapon widely used for anti-aircraft defence on all types of warships, from U-Boats to battleships. Its rate of fire, however, was relatively low and so, as with the U-Boats, on E-Boats it was soon replaced by the improved MG C/38. This weapon was magazine-fed with a cyclic rate of fire of around 240rpm and a range of more than 12,000m.

Eventually, as mentioned above, the forward machine gun was also replaced by a 2cm MG C/38, and this was followed by the fitting of a twin 2cm mount on the aft Flak platform. Yet even this improvement was considered inadequate by most boat commanders, and as a result a small number of selected boats in 2., 4., 5. and 6. Schnellbootsflottillen were armed with captured 4cm Bofors guns, in addition to the 2cm Flak armament.

E-BOAT EVOLUTION

S 14 Type (a)

Eleven examples of this type were built. The first four were equipped with what turned out to be unreliable MAN diesels so the remainder of the type had Daimler-Benz engines fitted. The two types of boat were visually similar to one another, only the power plant differing significantly. She wears the typical very pale grey livery of the period and carries her pennant number on the bow. Note also the large eagle and swastika national emblem carried on the side of her superstructure near the bridge. These emblems were removed shortly after the beginning of the war and placed in safe storage. Unlike the earlier boats, by the time this type entered service, four torpedoes rather than two were carried.

S 26 Type (b)

Built, like all the predecessor types, by Lürssen of Bremen-Vegesack, this type was 35m in length and displaced 110 tonnes. Powered by three Daimler-Benz 20-cylinder marine diesel engines, they could achieve a speed of 41 knots. Note that the torpedo tubes are now enclosed and the boats have a raised forecastle. Normally, operational boats had canvas 'dodgers' draped over the ship's rails to afford the crews some measure of protection from spray.

By late 1944, the gun armament was standardized at one 2cm MG C/38 forward, two twin 2cm Flak guns amidships and a 4cm or 3.7cm Flak gun astern. In a few cases, quadruple 2cm *Flakvierling* mounts were fitted astern, giving some boats a fairly hefty armament of 10 × 2cm cannon. Though impressive on paper, the penetrating power of the 2cm was poor, leading to them being contemptuously referred to as 'doorknockers' by the Germans.

S 30 Type (c)

A total of 16 of this type were built, using the smaller 16-cylinder Daimler-Benz engines, and thus able to achieve a top speed of 36 knots, only slightly lower than the S 26 Type. Up to six torpedoes could be carried (two in the tubes and four reloads) but the additional armament was still quite modest, with one 2cm Flak gun plus machine guns. Note the very distinctive upswept edge to the rear of the fairing around the torpedo tube. This example bears a distinctive but effective disruptive camouflage pattern and has the flotilla emblem of 1. Schnellbootsflottille, an eagle grasping a torpedo.

S 100 Type (d)

This was the most effective type and the type built in the greatest number. Manufacture was shared between Lürssen and Schlichting of Travemünde. These boats were 35m in length and displaced 110 tonnes. Powered by the 20-cylinder version of the Daimler-Benz engine, they could achieve 41 knots. Later boats were built with an armoured bridge (earlier builds were also upgraded with this feature) and in addition to its torpedos, this type carried a powerful gun armament – typically a 2cm gun in the bow, twin 2cm guns amidships and either a 3.7cm Flak, 4cm Bofors or quadruple 2cm *Flakvierling* on the aft mount. This example carries the black panther emblem of 4. Schnellbootsflottille.

Torpedoes

The main armament of the E-Boats was, of course, the torpedo. All E-Boats carried two bow tubes, with two spare torpedoes carried in racks on deck just behind the tubes, from where they could be quickly loaded. The standard torpedo carried was the 53.3cm G7a. Some 7.2m in length and weighing in at 1,530kg, the G7a was a steam-driven weapon. Its single propeller drove it along at a maximum speed of 44 knots to

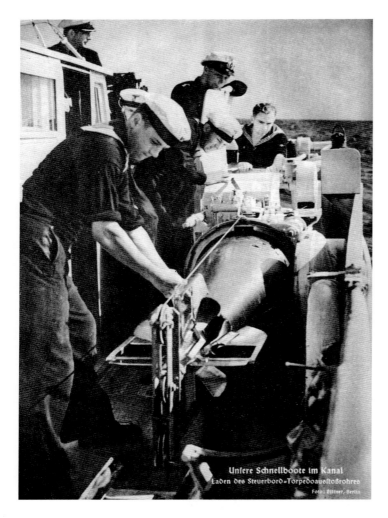

Unfere Schnellboote im Kanal
Laden des Steuerbord=Torpedoausstoßrohres
Foto: Bittner, Berlin

This interesting shot from a period propaganda publication shows E-Boat crewmen loading a torpedo into its tube. (Author's collection)

a range of 6,000m. At its optimum lower speed of 30 knots, its range extended to 14,400m. In the nose of the torpedo was the warhead, typically with 280kg of mixed explosive: Trinitrotoluene (TNT), Hexanitrophenylamine (HND) and powdered aluminium. Into the warhead was set a detonator with a small propeller. This propeller was in effect a timing mechanism, which charged the detonator whilst spinning, as the torpedo sped through the water. The detonator would not fully charge until it had covered about 30m, ensuring against premature detonation damaging the boat that had launched it. The detonator on the G7a was a contact type, activated by physical contact with the target.

Around half the length of the torpedo was taken up by a compressed-air cylinder. This was followed by a fuel tank and a combustion chamber in which the air and fuel mix was ignited to produce superheated steam, the steam driving a small four-cylinder engine that in turn powered the torpedo's propeller. Exhaust gases were vented through the hollow bore of the prop-shaft. The torpedo was fitted with a gyroscope linked to the rudders to ensure it kept on course, and a depth gauge that controlled its dive planes. Overall the G7a was an extremely expensive item, costing well over 20,000 Reichsmarks each, and was a highly sensitive piece of equipment. Fortunately for the E-Boats, its use on a surface ship was not beset by quite the same level of technical problems as was suffered by the U-Boat arm when launching the torpedo from a submarine.

The more advanced electrically driven G7e, widely used on U-Boats, was not carried by E-Boats. A number of advanced long-range torpedoes – the T3d – were used in limited numbers by E-Boats attacking the Allied bridgehead in Normandy. The T3d had a range of up to 57,000m, but at a slow speed of just 9 knots, and carried a 281kg warhead. Its range allowed the E-Boats to fire off their torpedoes from a safe distance. The torpedoes would run true until reaching the target area, after which they would circle until hitting a target. The T5 homing torpedo was also used by E-Boats in the latter part of the war, but without significant results.

Mines

Mines were another very important addition to the armoury of the E-Boats. The RMA and RMB types were the principal mines, though captured Russian-made MO8 mines were also deployed. The torpedo-tube launched TMB, as used in the U-Boat arm, was also used to good effect by the E-Boats, as were LMB and LMF types; both these latter types could be fitted with an acoustic or a magnetic trigger. A good number of the sinkings achieved by E-Boats were by the use of mines.

Radar

Radar was never successfully introduced into the S-Bootwaffe on a large scale. Although a few individual boats had radar sets fitted on an experimental basis, there was never any attempt to fit radar sets as standard, principally because none had been developed that were totally suitable for use on such craft.

This bow shot of an E-Boat entering port gives a good view of the outer doors on the enclosed torpedo tubes of later high-forecastle boats, and also shows the 2cm forward cannon in its special tub. (Bundesarchiv)

What were used, with some success, were passive radar receivers, which detected radar transmissions from enemy ships and thus at least alerted the E-Boats to the enemy presence. The primitive 'Biscay Cross' wire-wrapped wooden antennae, first used on U-Boats, were put to use on some E-Boats in late 1942. Later improved versions such as 'Samos' and 'Naxos', also developed for use on U-Boats, were fitted to several boats, but even in late 1944 many boats still had no such equipment fitted.

British vessels did have the advantage of radar equipment, and could thus track the German movements with relative ease. In order to confuse enemy radar, therefore, the E-Boats made use of two further pieces of equipment developed for use in U-Boats: the 'Thetis' decoy buoy and the 'Aphrodite' balloon. The latter was a helium-filled balloon from which dangled strips of foil. Anchored by a short cable, the 'Aphrodite' returned a strong radar 'signature' intended to attract enemy attention and allow the E-Boats to avoid detection.

THE MTB
CONFIGURATION AND ARMAMENT

Typical layout for British boats was to have the forward area taken up by crew accommodation, with the radio room and magazine below the bridge. The main fuel tanks were located amidships and the bulk of the after part of the boat below decks was taken up by the engine room. Further fuel tanks were located right at the stern.

MACHINE GUNS

Two types of .303in machine gun were typically carried. The Lewis Mk I used a 47- or 97-round drum magazine and had a rate of fire of 5,500rpm. It had a muzzle velocity of 746mps and an effective range of some 800m. From 1940 onwards, the

E-BOAT ARMAMENT

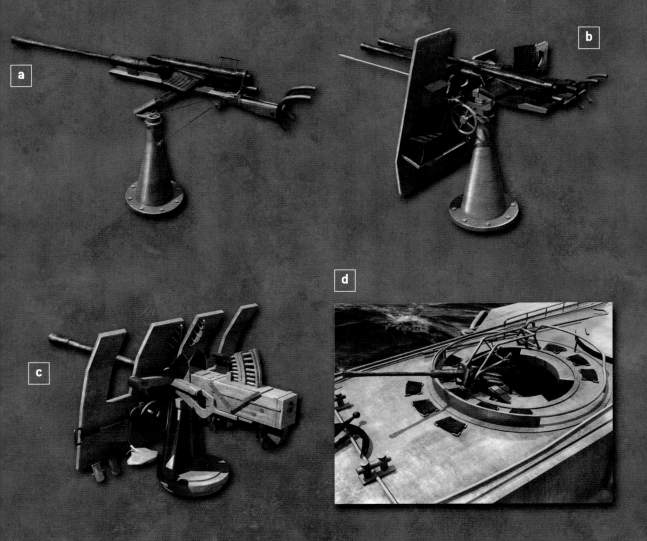

Typical armament on early E-Boats was the **2cm MG C/30 Flak (a)**, capable of sustained fire at 120rpm and with an effective range of around 2,400m. A similar weapon was used for anti-aircraft defence on early U-Boats.
The MG C/38 Flak (b) provided improved firepower by the simple expedient of pairing two 2cm guns in a twin mount, resulting in an increased rate of fire of 220rpm. Note that one barrel is mounted vertically and the other horizontally.

The heavy armament on later E-Boats was the **3.7cm/69 M42 Flak (c)**. This weapon could fire 250rpm with an effective range of 2,000m and a maximum range of around 6,400m.
A special version of the 2cm MG Flak was made solely for use on the bow gun position of later-model E-Boats. Known as the ***Drehkranzlafette* (d)**, it featured a very distinctive pantograph-style mount for the gun-sight.
It was manned by a crew of two.

MTB ARMAMENT

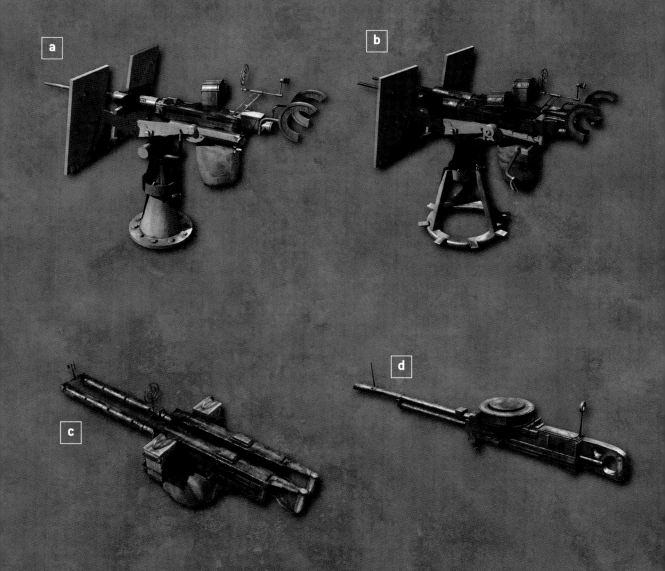

Analogous to the 2cm Flak weapons carried on E-Boats, the **20mm Oerlikon (a)** could fire at a rate of up to 450rpm and had a range of around 2,000m. Up to 100 rounds could be carried in a drum magazine as opposed to only 20 rounds in the magazine for the 2cm Flak guns. Like the 2cm Flak, the Oerlikon was also produced in a **twin version (b)**, allowing this weapon to deliver a much greater rate of fire than its German counterpart.

The **.30cal Browning machine gun (c)** was an American design that was widely used by other Allied nations during World War II. It could fire up to 600rpm with an effective range of 1,300m.

The **.303in Vickers K machine gun (d)**, originally designed for aircraft use, was also used as a shipboard weapon. It featured a distinctive drum magazine atop the weapon and could fire at a rate of 800rpm with a muzzle velocity of 762mps and an effective range of 2,000m.

Space was at a premium on an MTB, but these crewmen have managed to find themselves some room on the after deck to relax with some board games. (BAE Systems Surface Ships South, late Vosper Thornycroft Shipbuilding)

Lewis gun began to be replaced by the .303in Vickers Mk 1 No. 5. It used a 100-round drum magazine and fired at a faster rate of 950rpm. Muzzle velocity was around 730mps with an effective range of 2,000m.

The Vickers firm also produced the .5in machine gun used on many MTBs. With its water-filled cooling jacket and conical flash eliminator, the Vickers was a distinctive-looking weapon, often carried in a twin mount. It was belt-fed from a 650-round box magazine and fired at a rate of 700rpm. Muzzle velocity was 768mps.

HEAVY WEAPONS

Three basic calibres of heavier weapon were carried on British MTBs/MGBs: 20mm, 40mm and 57mm.

20mm Oerlikon

Originally a German design subsequently developed in Switzerland, the 20mm Oerlikon saw widespread use in both the Royal Navy and US Navy in both single-barrel and twin-barrel mounts. A 600-round drum magazine was used, with the weapon firing at a rate of 480rpm. Muzzle velocity was 830mps and effective range around 1,000m.

40mm Bofors

The 40mm Bofors gun was a Swedish design and one that, ironically, ended up being used on some E-Boats as well as on their British counterparts. Ammunition was contained in a four-round clip and was fired at a cyclical rate of 160rpm. Muzzle velocity was 880mps and range was up to 10,000m.

2pdr (40mm) Vickers Quick-Firing (QF) Mk VIII

Widely known as the 'Pom-Pom' due to the sound made when fired, this cannon was mounted as the forward weapon on many British boats. A four-round clip was used, and the gun fired at a rate of 115rpm. Muzzle velocity was 731mps and effective range 3,960m.

6pdr (57mm) QF Mk IIA

In the late stages of the war, some British boats were fitted with an even heavier weapon, the 6pdr QF Mk IIA. Originally developed as a tank gun, this weapon could fire at a rate of 40rpm. Muzzle velocity was 655mps and the range 5,700m. No boats with this armament, however, entered service in time to be sent into action against Germany's E-Boats before the war ended.

TORPEDOES

Two types of torpedo were carried on British MTBs: the 18in and the 21in.

18in Mk VIII Torpedo

At 5.3m in length, the Mk VIII weighed around 817kg, the explosive charge contributing 247kg of Torpex to the overall weight. Driven by a steam-turbine motor, the Mk VIII had a maximum range of 3,200m.

21in Mk XV Torpedo

The larger Mk XV was some 6.6m in length and weighed 1,565kg with the explosive charge being either 327kg of TNT or 365kg of Torpex. Also driven by a steam turbine, it had a much greater maximum range than the Mk VIII, at 6,400m.

Shown here is MTB 380, one of the larger 73ft Vospers, now equipped with four rather than two torpedo tubes and a twin 20mm Oerlikon mount on the forecastle. They could also carry machine-gun mounts on the torpedo tubes. (BAE Systems Surface Ships South, late Vosper Thornycroft Shipbuilding)

THE STRATEGIC SITUATION

After the fall of France in 1940, Germany became firmly ensconced along the Channel ports of France, Holland and Belgium, as well as in bases in occupied Norway. The situation faced by Britain was grim. Without essential supplies brought in by sea, Britain could not possibly survive. The Channel ports gave Admiral Dönitz and his U-Boats direct access to the Atlantic and his submarine commanders were soon inflicting devastating losses on trans-Atlantic shipping, even after the introduction of the convoy system. Britain was desperate for munitions to supply its armed forces, foodstuffs to feed its population and fuel to power its industries.

Even those battered convoys of merchant vessels which *had* successfully evaded the U-Boats on their way across the Atlantic, would then have to run the gauntlet of attacks from E-Boats, or minefields deployed by the same, as they approached the British coast. The Thames Estuary was particularly targeted by the E-Boats, whose commanders were keen to prevent supplies of food and fuel being landed directly into the capital.

As the war progressed, not only merchant shipping faced danger from the E-Boats. In addition, any attempt to launch an invasion of occupied Europe would require sending large numbers of ships across the narrow waters of the Channel, where they would be in real danger of attack by the fast and powerfully armed E-Boats.

Britain's own Coastal Forces were of course intent on inflicting the same sort of damage on Axis shipping, though coastal convoys in the Channel waters were somewhat less essential to Germany's survival than Allied shipping was to Britain. Each side's small coastal craft were primarily intended for actions against the other's merchant shipping, having insufficient protection against gunfire from heavier

A fine wartime study of one of the early E-Boat types. The boat number painted in black at the bow has been obscured by the censor. In fact, there was very little in the way of visual difference between the boats numbered from S 7 to S 25. (Author's collection)

warships, though inevitably E-Boats on one side and MTBs/MGBs on the other would see close-quarter combat against each other.

Although, initially, E-Boats were not only larger but more heavily armed than their British counterparts, necessitating gun boats (MGBs) being used to protect torpedo boats (MTBs), the latter gradually had their firepower increased to the stage that, though still smaller and lighter, they would have sufficient firepower to take on E-Boats without the need for extra support. Even in the early stages of the war, however, it soon became clear that the more daring and aggressive MTB commanders were perfectly capable of taking on, and besting, the more powerful E-Boats.

Early MTBs at sea. These boats – MTB 100 and MTB 102 – were 68ft VPV ('Vosper Private Venture') craft bought by the Royal Navy and classed as MTBs. Note that only MTB 102 at this time has been fitted with external torpedo tubes. (BAE Systems Surface Ships South, late Vosper Thornycroft Shipbuilding)

THE COMBATANTS

ORGANIZATION OF THE S-BOOTWAFFE

The E-Boats had originally fallen under the command of Führer der Torpedoboote (F.d.T., or Flag Officer Torpedo Boats), though it should be pointed out that here 'torpedo boats' related to the larger vessels that more resembled small destroyers. In 1942, the large torpedo boats passed to the command of the Führer der Zerstörer (F.d.Z., or Flag Officer Destroyers), and the Kriegsmarine's E-Boat forces came under the control of the newly appointed Führer der Schnellboote (F.d.S., or Flag Officer S-Boats).

E-Boats were organized into flotillas, of which there were eventually a total of 14. They ultimately operated in four main theatres, the English Channel/North Sea, the Baltic/Far North, the Black Sea and the Mediterranean/Aegean. Some E-Boats were committed for use in the Baltic during the invasion of Poland, but so quickly was the Polish Navy subdued that they saw little or no action.

The following flotillas are of interest to this work, having served on the Channel coast and seen action against their British counterparts:

1. S-Bootsflottille (with tenders[1] *Tsingtau, Carl Peters*)
2. S-Bootsflottille (with tenders *Tanga, Tsingtau*)
3. S-Bootsflottille (with tender *Adolf Lüderitz*)
4. S-Bootsflottille (with tenders *Tsingtau, Hermann von Wissmann*)
5. S-Bootsflottille (with tenders *Tsingtau, Hermann von Wissmann, Carl Peters*)

---

[1] E-Boat tenders were basically depot ships that ranged in size from those simply providing workshop facilities for repairs and maintenance to larger vessels that could also provide crew accommodation facilities. Tenders could be moved from flotilla to flotilla as required.

6. S-Bootsflottille (with tenders *Tsingtau, Tanga, Carl Peters, Adolf Lüderitz*)
7. S-Bootsflottille
8. S-Bootsflottille (with tenders *Tsingtau, Adolf Lüderitz*)
9. S-Bootsflottille (with tender *Tsingtau*)
10. S-Bootsflottille
11. S-Bootsflottille

The E-Boat tender *Tsingtau*, the support ship of at various points of 1., 2., 4., 5., 6., 8. and 9. S-Bootsflottillen operating on the Channel coast. (Author's collection)

Although relatively small, the E-Boat force was highly successful, and became a real threat to Allied shipping. A total of 23 Knight's Crosses of the Iron Cross were awarded to flotilla commanders and individual E-Boat commanders. Of these, eight particularly proficient E-Boat men, who had been decorated with the Oakleaves to the Knight's Cross, were also decorated with the *Schnellbootskriegsabzeichen* (E-Boat War Badge) with Diamonds, a personal gift from the commander-in-chief of the navy in recognition of their exceptional achievements. (Nine small diamonds were set into the swastika of a standard E-Boat War Badge, and the badge itself was made of gilded silver.)

It is interesting to note that the E-Boat War Badge awarded to E-Boat crews after their third combat sortie was unique amongst such badges, in that it was specifically redesigned to reflect new developments in E-Boat construction. The first badge, instituted in May 1941, depicted one of the early high forecastle types, but still with the relatively high cabin-type bridge. In 1943, a second type was introduced. The commander of 2. S-Bootsflottille, Kapitän zur See Rudolf Petersen, was involved in producing the design for this second version, which shows the later, sleeker type with the armoured bridge in a depiction that also imparts a greater impression of speed to the boat.

RIGHT
The award document for
the E-Boat War Badge of
a *Maschinenmaat* (Junior
Engineering Mate) with 5.
S-Bootsflottille. The badge
was awarded during the
period the unit was serving
on the Channel coast.
(Erik Krogh)

BELOW
The diagram shows a typical
attack formation, with E-Boats
approaching an enemy
convoy in pairs, or *Rotte*,
in line abreast. On drawing
near to their targets, the boats
spread out and begin their
attack run. After launching
their torpedoes, each column
of boats branches off in
opposite directions and
the boats either make their
escape from the area, or
reload their torpedo tubes to
make a second attack run.

E-BOAT TACTICS

E-Boats would typically use a line astern formation when on patrol, with the formation commander leading. On approaching the enemy, the unit then would move to line abreast, with the formation lining up to port or starboard of the lead boat, or dividing to line up either side with the lead boat in the centre. On drawing close to the enemy at full speed, the formation would split into two groups, to divide any enemy defensive fire. After launching their torpedoes at the targets, each group would then race through the enemy formation, with one group breaking to port and one to starboard as they sped away.

Like their British counterparts, E-Boats would not waste torpedoes in attacks on MTBs/MGBs, only on larger targets, instead relying on their considerable cannon armament against their enemy equivalents.

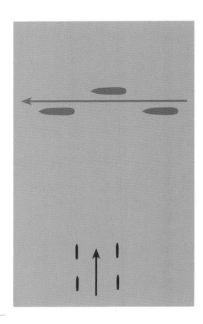

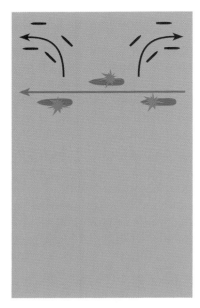

Neither the MTB nor the E-Boat was designed primarily for action against the other, but against merchant ships. In the course of their operations, however, they did indeed come to blows, in much the same way that fighter aircraft, often focused on shooting down enemy bombers, would inevitably end up engaging their opposite numbers who were present to defend the bombers.

During operations in the Channel, E-Boats developed a tactic known as *Stichansatz* ('Random Approach'). This involved the flotilla heading towards the anticipated route of the enemy formation at right angles to the direction of enemy travel. Approximately 16km from the planned interception point, the flotilla would then disperse in line abreast, in two-boat *Rotten*, with a distance of approximately 3km between each *Rotte*,

Early (left) and late versions of the E-Boat War Badge, specifically redesigned to reflect the sleeker appearance of the later armoured bridge type boats. (Author's collection)

Here we see further typical battle formations for an E-Boat unit. In formation 'A' we see the patrol formation in line astern; 'L' indicates the formation leader. The boats operate in pairs known as *Rotte*, with each pair having a lead boat, or *Rottenführer* – indicated by an 'R' – and a 'slave' boat, the equivalent to a pilot's 'wingman', indicated by an 'S'. The options once moving from patrol formation to attack formation include: formation 'B', lining up in line abreast with the formation leader in the middle of the formation; formation 'C', line abreast to starboard, with the formation leader to the left; and formation 'D', line abreast to port, with the formation leader to the right.

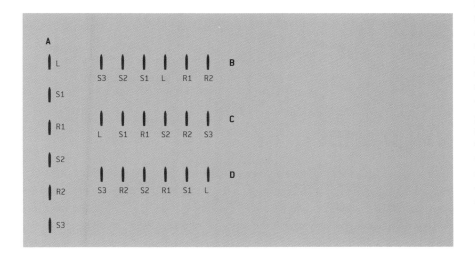

and slowly approach the final attack position, where they would simply stop and await the arrival of the enemy. If no enemy appeared, the whole formation would move forward 3–5km, to allow for a margin of error in the original course calculated for the enemy. This tactic was not always successful, though on occasions when an enemy convoy was intercepted using this method, significant results were achieved.

ORGANIZATION OF BRITISH COASTAL FORCES

The Coastal Forces Command of the Royal Navy was established in 1940 under the command of Rear-Admiral P.K. Kekewich, with his headquarters initially at the shore base HMS *Attack* in Portland and later in London. Various subordinate commands were located around Great Britain, with those most important to the battles in the Channel being Captain Coastal Forces Nore Command at Chatham and Captain Coastal Forces (Channel) in Portsmouth.

Under these commands were various bases (all, in the British tradition, given ships' names despite being on land). As was the case with their German counterparts, flotillas were not necessarily permanently located at a specific location and could be moved from base to base as operational requirements dictated. The bases included:

Bases	Location	Types of vessel
HMS *Beehive*	Felixstowe	MTBs, MGBs and MLs
HMS *Cicala*	Dartmouth	MTBs and MLs
HMS *Dartmouth II*	Dartmouth	MTBs, MGBs and MLs
HMS *Fervent*	Ramsgate	MTBs, MGBs and MLs
HMS *Midge*	Yarmouth	MTBs, MGBs and MLs
HMS *Minos*	Lowestoft	MTBs, MGBs and MLs
HMS *Minos II*	Lowestoft	MTBs, MGBs and MLs
HMS *Vernon*	Portsmouth	MTBs
HMS *Wasp*	Dover	MTBs, MGBs and MLs

MTB TACTICS

Typically, MTBs on operations would engage the enemy at night and use one of two formations: line astern or a 'V' formation, with the formation commander in the lead positions. Both formations had advantages and disadvantages. In line astern it was simple for following boats to match the direction of travel of the boat immediately in front, but more difficult to detect changes in speed of the lead boat in order to keep the distance between boats steady at around 60m. In a 'V' formation, it is somewhat easier to maintain position and spot changes of speed in the boat in front, but slightly more difficult to quickly spot small changes in course.

Typically, the boats would cruise at around 25 knots, this being the optimum speed to allow maximum operational range and minimize fuel consumption. On spotting enemy ships, the boats dropped their speed to around 9 knots in order to attempt to approach the enemy quietly and avoid tell-tale bow waves, hopefully remaining undetected for as long as possible. Boats would also often manoeuvre into a favourable attack position then cut engines and sit in silence in the darkness until the enemy ships crossed in front of them.

Ideal attack positions for MTBs (and E-Boats) were little different to those for submarines. Although an approach from astern was often used, an actual attack from this position was less likely to be successful as the narrow, beam aspect would offer a smaller target, whereas an attack from port or starboard beam opened up the whole length of the vessel to aim for. The formation would then typically split into two to make its attack, each element approaching from a different direction to improve the chances of hitting the targets should they attempt evasive manoeuvres. Torpedoes, of course, would only be used against merchant vessels or large warships – the depth at which torpedoes ran, and the speed of the small combat craft, precluding their use against E-Boats. Against these, the principal weapons would be the MTB's machine guns and cannon.

After hitting the enemy, the MTBs used speed as their principal tool to avoid retribution from the more heavily armed E-Boats, making off at top speed whilst generating a smokescreen from smoke-pots near the stern. Once out of danger, speed would once again be reduced to the normal cruising speed of around 25 knots.

MGBs were often used in joint operations with MTBs, their heavier armament providing defence for the lightly armed MTBs if attacked or pursued by E-Boats. As the war progressed however, MTBs were gradually given heavier armament and were far better equipped to defend themselves against their German counterparts.

Stern view of MTB 380. Although the complement of torpedo tubes was increased from two to four, they were the smaller 18in tubes compared to 21in tubes on the earlier boats. (BAE Systems Surface Ships South, late Vosper Thornycroft Shipbuilding)

COMBAT

1939–40: FIRST COMBAT

Unlike the Germans, the British were totally unprepared for coastal operations by small, fast and relatively cheap warships. On the outbreak of war, Germany possessed just over 60 E-Boats and R-Boats, whilst Britain had only nine small coastal craft, of which five were actually sub-chasers and one was an experimental boat, leaving just three purpose-built MTBs. For the time being, Britain would have no effective answer to the threat to its coastal shipping in the waters of the southern North Sea and the English Channel.

E-Boat operations in the first part of the war consisted mainly of blockade work in the Bay of Danzig during the campaign against Poland, followed by the support of Operation *Weserübung*, the invasion of Norway and Denmark. Although the E-Boats would see action against British warships around this period, including damaging the destroyer HMS *Kelly*, it would not be until the *Westfeldzug* ('campaigns in the West') of May 1940 that E-Boats would begin their regular attacks on Allied shipping in the waters in and around the English Channel.

The very first sortie in the Channel came on 15 May 1940, when a small steamer was sunk by an E-Boat operating from the German island of Borkum. Around this same time, the very first British flotillas in its Coastal Forces were being formed, with 1, 4 and 10 MTB Flotillas in Felixstowe having a grand total of five, eight and five boats respectively.

The weak British Coastal Forces spent much of their first few months in action clearing mines deposited by their German opposite numbers. Soon E-Boats were operating out of captured ports, however, and the first major German success came on 29 May when S 30, operating from Den Helder in occupied Holland under the command of Oberleutnant zur See Wilhelm Zimmermann, torpedoed and sank the destroyer HMS *Wakeful* with heavy British loss of life – the warship had been carrying troops evacuated from Dunkirk. On the same night, S 34 sank the merchant ship *Aboukir* off the English coast, and just one day later, S 23 under Leutnant Georg Christiansen and S 26 under Leutnant Kurt Fimmen – also from 1. S-Bootsflottillen – attacked and sank the French destroyer *Siroco*. Like HMS *Wakeful*, the *Siroco* was also carrying a heavy load of rescued British and French troops from the beaches at Dunkirk, and as well as many of the ship's crew, almost 500 troops were lost.

MTBs and MLs also saw much action during the evacuation of Allied troops. MTBs 22, 24 and 25 from 4 MTB Flotilla provided escort and reconnaissance for destroyers involved in evacuating both civil and military British personnel from Holland, whilst MTB 16 from 1 MTB Flotilla evacuated a number of both British and Dutch personnel. On 24 May, MTBs 15 and 16 were involved in providing escort for an unsuccessful attempt to sink concrete-filled blockships in the harbour at Zeebrugge. A further attempt on 26 May, this time with MTBs 14 and 15 providing escort, achieved its operational goals.

Meanwhile, boats from 1 MTB Flotilla would provide a defensive screen in an attempt to prevent E-Boats attacking the evacuation fleet at Dunkirk, whilst MTB 102 was involved in ferrying evacuees from the beaches out to the destroyers in deeper waters offshore. It was MTB 107 that had the distinction of being the last Allied boat to leave Dunkirk before it fell. The little craft motored around, picking up the last few stragglers from the beaches, constantly under enemy fire, before making her way safely back across the Channel.

The collapse of the opposition to the German forces in France and the Low Countries, and the acquisition of several Channel ports, then gave the E-Boats ideal bases from which to operate in actions against the British coastal convoys. The freighter *Roseburn* was sunk on the night of 19 June in an attack by S 19 and S 26. The first significant anti-convoy operation came on 23 June, however, when six E-boats attacked a small British convoy off Dungeness, S 19 sinking the small coaster *Kingfisher* and S 36 destroying the larger tanker *Albuera*.

BOTTOM LEFT
MTB 102 at speed. Displacing 32 tonnes, she had a very respectable top speed of 40 knots. MTB 102 took part in the evacuation at Dunkirk. She survived the war, was preserved and is still in running order today. (BAE Systems Surface Ships South, late Vosper Thornycroft Shipbuilding)

BOTTOM RIGHT
Before having external torpedo tubes fitted either side of her wheelhouse, MTB 102 had a single internal centrally mounted torpedo tube that fired though an opening in her bow. (BAE Systems Surface Ships South, late Vosper Thornycroft Shipbuilding)

By late June, 10 MTB Flotilla had been assigned to air-sea rescue duties in the Thames Estuary, whilst 11 MTB Flotilla in Dover was involved in anti-E-Boat patrols in the Straits of Dover, as well as rescuing those either shot down in aerial battles or who had survived the sinking of their ships. On 22 June the E-Boats suffered their first loss of the war, when S 32 hit a mine west of Boulogne and was so badly damaged that she sank soon afterwards. A subsequent E-Boat operation three days later, by boats from 1. S-Bootsflottille, had mixed results. One large freighter was sunk and two damaged, but one E-Boat also sustained heavy damage. Over the next few weeks, minor successes were achieved with a few small coasters being sunk, but on 25 July an attack on Convoy CW8 saw three British merchant ships sunk and a further attack, this time on Convoy CW9, resulted in the sinking of three freighters with two others damaged.

Sadly, one ship hit by torpedoes from S 27 around this time was the French liner *Meknes*. This passenger vessel was in fact repatriating more than 1,000 French troops home from Britain to France after the French signing of an armistice with Germany, and as a non-belligerent, should not have been attacked. It appears, however, that neither the Vichy French government, nor the Germans, had been contacted to advise them of this specific repatriation and arrange safe passage. On the night of 24 July, S 27 fired four torpedoes at a large merchantman, missed, but one of the torpedoes continued past its intended target and struck the *Meknes*.

On 8 August 1940, E-Boats from 1. S-Bootsflottille attacked a coastal convoy consisting of 21 ships, mostly small freighters and colliers, which were in transit through the Straits of Dover. Eleven vessels from the convoy were either sent to the bottom or severely damaged. One of the most significant successes for the E-Boats during this period came on 4 September, when a convoy was intercepted off the British coast and five freighters were sunk with a further freighter damaged. The flotilla returned to Germany in October.

Meanwhile, 2. S-Bootsflottille operating out of Ostend had been involved principally in mine-laying operations rather than anti-convoy sorties. Any major operations by this unit had been rendered infeasible when the torpedo depot blew up in mid-August and several boats were severely damaged in the resulting conflagration. The arrival of 3. S-Bootsflottille at Vlissingen in September did little to help matters, as most of the boats involved were elderly examples with poor reliability, on top of which most were damaged in an air raid the day after they arrived. By 1 November, the flotilla had just two serviceable boats available.

This E-Boat at high speed was shown in a wartime propaganda magazine. The pre-war boat number has been painted over, though she still carries the eagle and swastika emblem on the hull on each side of the bridge. These were removed shortly after the start of the war. (Author's collection)

40

Although the MTBs so far had been involved mostly in defensive operations, such as mine-clearing and rescue missions, in September 1940 two boats from 1 MTB Flotilla in Felixstowe joined in an attack on an enemy convoy (the attack had already been launched by destroyers out of Harwich); the MTBs succeeded in sinking an ammunition ship.

In one attack in October 1940, MTB 31 was one of two Felixstowe boats that encountered an enemy convoy in the Schelde estuary. After experiencing problems with the torpedo-firing mechanisms, the boat ran straight at an enemy ship, actually scraping its side, to drop depth charges under its bows before speeding off!

On 1 November, 1. S-Bootsflottille was temporarily transferred to Bergen in Norway, leaving only 2. and 3. S-Bootsflottillen covering the Channel, 3. S-Bootsflottille at this point having only two serviceable boats remaining. The arrival of an additional boat in mid-November allowed 3. S-Bootsflottille to recommence operations, but unfortunately for the flotilla, the newly arrived boat was sunk by enemy destroyers a few days after its arrival.

The return of four boats from 1. S-Bootsflottille in mid-December finally gave the Germans sufficient resources to mount a major action, and on 23 December 1940 a combined operation off Great Yarmouth involving 1., 2. and 3. S-Bootsflottillen saw a successful attack on a convoy escorted by destroyers. Whilst the firepower of the destroyers managed to drive off most of the E-Boats, a few slipped through the escorts and sank two merchant ships, the Dutch vessel *Stad Maastricht* and the trawler *Pelton*. During the operation two E-Boats – S 28 and S 29 – collided, something that would happen with disturbing regularity during high-speed attacks on convoys, with boats jinking and manoeuvring to gain good firing positions whilst trying to avoid enemy fire.

Around this same time period, British Coastal Forces were forming up around the south coast. The 11 MTB Flotilla was based at Dover and the Nore Command, based around the Medway, had 1, 4 and 10 MTB Flotillas. Most of the operations mounted by these coastal craft involved supporting the evacuation of remnants of the British Expeditionary Force (BEF) from France. MTBs played a major part in air-sea rescue operations during the Battle of Britain, rescuing both RAF and Luftwaffe airmen who had been shot down over the waters of the Channel and the Thames Estuary. They were also involved in the rescue of seamen whose ships had been sunk by German aircraft and often put up defensive anti-aircraft fire when escorting convoys. Not unlike the E-Boats, MTBs were further used on mine-laying operations against German-held ports, and were responsible for more sinkings by this method than by torpedo attacks.

An E-Boat torpedo tube is loaded on one of the early models. The fact that the scene is unfolding at night is typical of the fact that E-Boats tended to operate under the cover of darkness when possible. (Author's collection)

Here we see the main E-Boat bases used for operations predominantly against British coastal shipping. The occupation of existing naval ports in France and the Low Countries gave the Germans ideal bases from which to conduct such operations. The narrow and often relatively shallow waters in the Channel area were perfect for the E-Boats, which could dash out from their heavily protected bases, often under the cover of darkness, attack shipping or lay mines and be back in port before the British could react. Daytime operations were much more dangerous, with the probability of attack from British aircraft being fairly high. The locations of the principal bases for the MTB/MGB flotillas opposing the Germans are also indicated. It was quite common for more than one type of boat (MGB, MTB, ML, etc.) to operate from the same port.

Significantly for the Royal Navy, in October 1940 its small coastal craft were finally gathered together formally under their own command, when Piers Kekewich was appointed as Rear-Admiral Coastal Forces. He began to build the units under his command from modest beginnings into what would eventually become a far bigger and more powerful force that Germany's S-Bootwaffe.

By the end of 1940, the E-Boat crews could look back on a relatively successful year, having sunk 26 enemy merchant vessels representing just under 50,000 tonnes, as well as sinking or badly damaging a further ten warships. This tally was achieved for the loss of just five E-Boats.

1941: THE BUILD-UP

The New Year started inauspiciously for the E-Boats. Not a single sinking was achieved in January, principally due to poor weather conditions, with heavy fog affecting visibility and providing good cover for the British coastal convoys.

On 6 February, however, the small coaster *Angularity* was sunk by boats from 2. S-Bootsflottille, whose crews obtained valuable intelligence information on convoy routes from survivors who were picked up. Subsequent operations by 1. S-Bootsflottille during February resulted in the sinking of the freighters *Algarve* and *Minorca* and the destroyer HMS *Exmoor*.

In the spring of 1941, attempts were made to improve inter-service cooperation between the Kriegsmarine and the Luftwaffe. Reconnaissance patrols were flown by Ju 88 aircraft, operating during daylight hours. On spotting a convoy, they would report its movements and shadow the ships until nightfall. E-Boats would then acquire an 'ambush' position from which they would launch an attack under the cover of darkness. Using this tactic, during the night of 7 March 1941 a combined force of 12 E-Boats from both 1. and 3. S-Bootsflottillen intercepted a convoy and sent seven merchants to the bottom, totalling some 13,000 tonnes.

On 17 April, boats from 3. S-Bootsflottille were preparing to launch an attack on a British convoy when they were attacked by three British MTBs. One of the German boats, S 58, suffered considerable damage, though she succeeded in making it back to base. Although the smaller and more lightly armed MTBs would not normally expect to inflict mortal damage on the bigger German vessels, their presence would certainly be enough to interfere with the E-Boats' attempts to make a successful attack run on the merchants in the convoy.

April would also see the first significant encounter between E-Boats and MGBs. During mine-laying sorties on the night of 29 April, boats from 1. and 2. S-Bootsflottillen came under attack by two British destroyers: HMS *Worcester* and HMS *Cotswold*. The E-Boats evaded the enemy under the cover of darkness and whilst manoeuvring to evade the enemy, ran into Convoy EC13. The E-Boats immediately attacked, sinking the merchant *Ambrose Fleming*, carrying a cargo of coal. On the same night, boats from 3. S-Bootsflottille were on a mine-laying mission near the Thames Estuary when they encountered MGB 59 and MGB 61 from 6 MGB Flotilla. A furious firefight developed which lasted almost half an hour, though no vessels from either side appear to have been sunk.

Given that E-Boats generally preferred to make their attacks under the cover of darkness, activity unsurprisingly tailed off somewhat during the long hours of daylight of the summer months. Both 1. and 2. S-Bootsflottillen were transferred to the Baltic, with 4. S-Bootsflottille under Kapitänleutnant Niels Bätge moving into the Channel area. This flotilla was based at first in Scheveningen, later moving briefly to Boulogne when new E-Boat bunkers there were completed, before ending up in Cherbourg, from where it launched mine-laying operations in English coastal waters.

Little was achieved by the new arrivals, however – the flotilla was still equipped with older E-Boat types, which were unreliable and prone to mechanical breakdowns.

One encounter between these older E-Boats and British MGBs took place on

Here we see the after deck on MTB 523, with a twin 20mm Oerlikon squeezed into the narrow space between the aft torpedo tubes. (BAE Systems Surface Ships South, late Vosper Thornycroft Shipbuilding)

This shot of the forward deck on MTB 523 affords a good view of the 6pdr quick-firing gun, affectionately known as the 'Pom-pom'. (BAE Systems Surface Ships South, late Vosper Thornycroft Shipbuilding)

20 June 1941, when S 20, S 22 and S 24 were subjected to a surprise attack by MGBs 58, 59 and 65 whilst engaged in mine-laying. The two sides lashed each other with cannon and machine-gun fire, but no major damage was done. Having disrupted the German operations, the MGBs sped off into the night.

In July, 4. S-Bootsflottille moved back to Boulogne, from where E-Boat operations were undertaken against targets detected by the *Freya* radar station at Cap Griz Nez. Such missions in August 1941 were indeed successful, with the radar stations detecting British shipping and the E-Boats sinking several merchant ships.

Moving back to Scheveningen again in mid-August, and still the only flotilla in the area, 4. S-Bootsflottille once again achieved positive results working in cooperation with the Luftwaffe – on 6 September its E-Boats joined Luftwaffe bombers in an attack on a convoy. Such cooperation was becoming rare, however, as the bulk of the Luftwaffe's strength was needed on the Eastern Front, the invasion of the Soviet Union leaving scant resources available for the Channel coast.

On 8 September 1941, MTBs 35 and 318 set out from Dover to intercept a small but heavily escorted German coastal convoy, with MTB 54 following later. After reaching the planned interception point, MTBs 35 and 318 succeeded in penetrating the convoy's protective screen of E-Boats, R-Boats and *Vorpostenboote* (VP-Boats – armed trawlers), each puttering along on only one engine to keep noise at a minimum. Due to the fast speed of the convoy, the MTBs then had to engage all of their engines and the great increase in noise alerted the enemy to their presence. All of the German warships, and even some coastal batteries, opened fire on the diminutive British boats as they manoeuvred to find a good firing position whilst avoiding enemy gunfire.

MTB 35 was completed in 1941 and operated out of Dover until she was retired from service in 1943. She carried two torpedo tubes and a twin .5in Vickers machine-gun mount in a tub just visible to the rear of the wheelhouse. (BAE Systems Surface Ships South, late Vosper Thornycroft Shipbuilding)

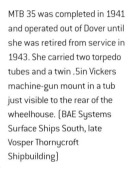

The interior of the wheelhouse on the early MTBs was a very cramped space indeed, as can be seen here on MTB 35. (BAE Systems Surface Ships South, late Vosper Thornycroft Shipbuilding)

Just as the Germans found their range, MTB 35 fired off a single torpedo, which struck the merchant ship at the end of the enemy column. MTB 318 fired off both her torpedoes, but the intended target was able to avoid them, so with her torpedoes expended she set off for home.

Once MTB 35 had escaped to a safe distance from the enemy convoy, it was discovered that the other torpedo had in fact misfired and was still in its tube. Just at this point, MTB 54 arrived with both torpedoes still available, so the two MTBs set off again in pursuit of the German convoy. Meanwhile, boats from 3 MGB Flotilla were attempting to achieve an ambush position ahead of the convoy, in order to engage and draw off the escorts so that the MTBs could renew their attack on the merchants.

The MGBs began their attack just after 1.00am and soon an intense battle was raging. The situation becoming so confused that some gunners on the German VP-Boats began firing at their own E-Boats, mistaking them for attacking MGBs. Just then, the two MTBs arrived and launched their torpedoes at the remaining German merchant vessel, which received direct hits and was soon ablaze and sinking. MTB 35, however, had been at the receiving end of some very heavy fire from several German boats. Part of her stern had been blown away and she was unable to steer.

The MGBs, unaware of her predicament, had set off for home after sinking an E-Boat and one of the VP-Boats, leaving MTB 35 badly damaged and facing the remaining VP-Boat and at least five E-Boats. Yet for some inexplicable reason, just as the crew were preparing to scuttle the MTB to prevent her capture, the enemy boats slowly formed up and motored away into the darkness, leaving the badly battered MTB to limp back across the Channel, whereupon she was beached at Ramsgate.

OVERLEAF

Our scene shows one of the earliest engagements between MTBs and E-Boats, which took place in the Thames Estuary on 17 April 1941. E-Boats from 3. Schnellbootsflottille had located a convoy and were preparing to attack under the cover of darkness. S 57 and S 58 were beginning their attack run when three MTBs came roaring out of the darkness with all guns blazing. The E-Boats were taken by surprise and suffered heavy damage. S 58, under the command of Leutnant zur See Geiger, was particularly badly hit, suffering damage to her hull and engine room. Given the relatively light armament carried by MTBs at this early point in the war, the fact that they showed themselves capable of damaging and driving off the much larger and heavier E-Boats was seen as a significant success, and provided a much-needed morale boost for the British.

On 9 October, four boats from 2. S-Bootsflottille returned to Rotterdam from the Baltic, and three days later the two flotillas launched a joint sortie against a convoy, which resulted in two merchant ships being sunk. By early October, a total of six boats from 2. S-Bootsflottille and four from 4. S-Bootsflottille were available for operations.

Although many significant successes were achieved, results were often mixed. During one attack on a convoy during the night of 19/20 November 1941, a formation of E-Boats from 2. S-Bootsflottille had been directed to a British convoy by Luftwaffe reconnaissance aircraft, and swiftly succeeded in sinking the merchants *Aruba* and *Waldinge* as well as the tanker *War Mehtar*. Whilst reforming for a second run, however, confused signals resulted in S 41 and S 47 colliding, with the former suffering serious damage. Whilst motoring along slowly with the damaged S 41 under tow, the Germans were then surprised by two British MGBs from 6 MGB Flotilla. MGB 63, MGB 64 and MGB 67 had set out from Felixstowe under the command of Lieutenant Commander Robert Hichens (on MGB 64) after receiving reports of the German attacks, though MGB 63 suffered engine failure and had to be left behind. The other two boats proceeded, attempting to intercept the E-Boats, and eventually spotted a group of five enemy boats. The British attacked immediately and with such vigour that the German boats sped off after a brief firefight. MGB 64 received some damage to its guns in the action. Shortly afterwards a lone E-Boat was also encountered, but managed to escape. Just as the British boats were about to give up their search for the enemy and return to port, the damaged S 41 was discovered, abandoned and left to sink slowly with its sea-cocks open after its crew had been rescued. Hichens' men boarded the E-Boat before it could sink and were able to recover valuable communications equipment and charts before S 41 eventually foundered. As commander of the British force, Hichens was awarded the Bar to his Distinguished Service Cross (DSC) for this action.

All of the other 2. S-Bootsflottille E-Boats had been shot up to some degree both by the MGBs and also by British aircraft, which intercepted them again on their way back to port, leaving only 4. S-Bootsflottille fully operational. What had begun as a positive sortie by the E-Boats had ended in disaster. The real success for the British force was in proving that the smaller British craft could engage and defeat a larger force of much heavier and better-armed E-Boats.

In the remaining few weeks of 1941, E-Boats from 4. S-Bootsflottille intercepted two further convoys. On 23 November they sank the *Virgilia* and the *Groenlo* from Convoy FS654, as well damaging the *Blairnevis*, and on 28 November they sank the *Cormarsh*, *Empire Newcomen* and the *Asperity* from a northbound convoy. The flotilla also carried out mine-laying operations with some of the 2. S-Bootsflottille boats, which had been repaired and were once again ready for operational use. Combined mine-laying operations between the two flotillas also paid dividends, with an estimated 12 ships totalling around 50,000 tonnes being lost to a large minefield laid between Orfordness and the Humber estuary on the south-east coast of England.

During 1941, therefore, the E-Boats had sunk a total of 29 merchant ships representing just under 59,000 tonnes, with many others damaged. On the British side, in the year since taking over his new command, Rear-Admiral Kekewich had built up his forces from around 80 boats operating out of five bases, to nearly 300 boats and 20 bases.

1942: SUCCESS FOR THE E-BOATS

Whilst the E-Boats' main targets were the coastal convoys travelling along the east coast of the UK, they were also heavily involved in providing protection for their own coastal convoys, as well as for returning blockade breakers and auxiliary cruisers. Up until the beginning of 1942, in fact, the greatest number of actions by both E-Boats and MTBs/MGBs were against enemy merchant vessels (using both torpedoes and mines) rather than against each other. During the whole of 1941, for example, only one MGB was sunk by an E-Boat and only one E-Boat was lost to an MGB.

Both sides had learned much from their experiences over the last two years. Though the early E-Boats had an advantage in speed and size over their British counterparts, and could carry a significant payload in terms of torpedoes and/or mines, their defensive armament was not particularly significant. That being said, defence against attacks by Allied aircraft does

Oberleutnant Karl Kunzel, commander, at various points in 1941–42, of E-Boats S 25, S 28, S 103 and S 108 in 1. S-Bootsflottille during its operations in the Channel. (Author's collection)

not seem to have been a particular problem in this early part of the war. For one thing, RAF fighters found the fast and agile E-Boats very difficult targets, and at this time rarely ever sank an E-Boat by aerial attack. On the other hand, the E-Boat, violently manoeuvring to avoid attack from the air, was hardly a stable gun mount from which to return effective anti-aircraft fire.

Both sides had identified shortcomings in their vessels. The early 2cm gun on some E-Boats was insufficiently powerful to do much damage to a vessel being pursued. The MGB/MTB types at this stage in the war had their most powerful armament astern, which was fine for defensive fire if they were themselves pursued, but also left them unable to inflict critical hits when they were chasing E-Boats.

The British had begun the war with two basic types of boat: the lightly armed, torpedo-carrying MTB whose prime purpose was, like the E-Boat, to attack enemy merchant shipping, and the more heavily armed MGB whose job was to intercept the E-Boats and protect the MTBs. Later E-Boats, with their upgraded armament and armoured bridges, would roll the two types of craft into one. The British would gradually adopt a similar policy by significantly upgrading the armament on their MTBs, giving them a fighting chance to take on an E-Boat on near-even terms. The MGBs' role as protector of the MTBs become less significant; indeed, some of them would have torpedo tubes added, further blurring the differences between the types.

ROBERT HICHENS

Lieutenant Commander Robert Hichens, DSO, DSC and Bar, with a German flag seized from the E-Boat he boarded. (Royal Navy)

Robert Peverell Hichens was born on 2 March 1909. He joined the Officer Training Corps whilst at university and was commissioned as a second lieutenant in the Territorial Army. He later applied for a transfer to the Royal Naval Volunteer Reserve (RNVR), however, and shortly after the beginning of the war became a sub-lieutenant in the RNVR. His initial wartime experience was with 4 and 5 Minesweeping Flotillas. Hichens was involved in the evacuation of Allied personnel from Dunkirk and volunteered to stay behind and help the rescue effort after his own ship left, knowing he would then have to get home himself. He did, in fact, make it back, and returned to Dunkirk a further three times to assist with the evacuation. For his efforts, he was awarded the Distinguished Service Cross (DSC).

A request for a transfer to Coastal Forces was approved and resulted in Hichens taking command of Motor Anti-Submarine Boat (MASB) 16 in November 1940. By September 1941, Hichens had been promoted to lieutenant commander, and he took command of 6 MGB Flotilla. On 19 November, shortly after taking over his new command, Hichens set off on the patrol that resulted in his capture of an E-Boat and the award of a Bar to his DSC. Another successful engagement with E-Boats on 19 December 1941 earned him a Mention in Despatches, and on 21 April 1942 a further victory against a superior enemy force earned him the Distinguished Service Order (DSO). Offered a promotion and transfer to a shore-based posting, Hichens declined and remained with his unit. On 12 April 1943, Hichens, on MGB 77, was hit by enemy fire during an attack on two enemy VP-Boats and was killed outright.

OPERATION *CERBERUS*

On 12 February 1942, E-Boats from 2., 4. and 6. S-Bootsflottillen were assigned as escorts during the so-called 'Channel Dash' (Operation *Cerberus*), when the German heavy warships *Scharnhorst*, *Gneisenau* and *Prinz Eugen*, plus other smaller warships, sailed from Brest in Brittany to their bases in Germany, via the English Channel.

The German formation escaped detection until it was off Le Touquet. Attacks on the German ships by air proved fairly ineffective due to a powerful Luftwaffe screening force, and so MTBs from 6 MTB Flotilla in Dover were despatched to attack the German ships as they passed through the Straits of Dover. The MTBs ran into a smokescreen laid by the E-Boats and other German coastal vessels. The outer screen, consisting of E-Boats, torpedo boats and destroyers, prevented the MTBs from getting too close to the heavy units. Thus the MTBs were forced to fire their torpedoes from

extreme range, never being able to get much closer than around 2,000m to the German capital ships, and were unable to determine whether any torpedoes had hit their intended targets (none had). Slightly further north, the MTBs based at Ramsgate had been involved in a heavy action the previous night and had only three boats available. This tiny force could have no real impact on the large and well-defended German force.

On 19 February, Convoy FS29 came under attack by E-Boats from 2. S-Bootsflottille, but the combined firepower of the two destroyers protecting the convoy, assisted by two MGBs and two MLs, was enough to drive off the attackers. As the E-Boats sped off, S 39 and S 53 collided at high speed. S 39 was able to proceed, but S 53 was partially flooded. The destroyer HMS *Holderness* approached with the intention of putting a boarding crew on the E-Boat and seizing her. As the destroyer drew near, however, S 53's commander, Oberleutnant zur See Peter Block, blew his vessel up to prevent her capture, sacrificing his own life in the process.

One particularly interesting engagement took place on 14 March 1942, when three MGBs – 87, 88 and 89 – under the command of Lieutenant J.B.R. Home, lay in wait off Ijmuiden. They were hoping to ambush a returning force of E-Boats that had been reported as active in the area, and which in fact had already sunk the destroyer HMS *Vortigern* during an attack on Convoy FS749 off Cromer.

The bulk of the E-Boat force had, unbeknown to the British, already returned to its base in Boulogne. Yet one boat, S 111, travelling alone, was intercepted by the British boats, which attacked at full speed and with all guns blazing. The Germans were so taken by surprise by the intense attack that the commander, Oberleutnant zur See Popp, and his bridge crew were killed and several other crew members jumped overboard. S 111 was the first E-Boat to be captured by the Royal Navy and was taken under tow. The German *Reichskriegsflagge* was quickly struck and the White Ensign was raised on S 111's flagstaff.

Before the British could enjoy the fruits of their success, however, the remainder of the German formation had been warned of the attack on their comrades. They rushed back to the scene and immediately attacked. Deciding that discretion was the

ABOVE LEFT
The single light 2cm Flak gun on its pedestal mount was a typical, if not particularly effective, feature of the armament of early E-Boats. The netting seen in this shot was to collect empty shell cases. (Hermann Büchting via R. Mills)

ABOVE RIGHT
Wearing special sun goggles, two E-Boat crewmen anxiously scan the skies, watching for Allied aircraft. (Hermann Büchting via R. Mills)

Looking towards the stern on a 70ft MTB. The machine-gun mounts can be seen atop the aft torpedo tube brackets, where they sit over the white bands. (BAE Systems Surface Ships South, late Vosper Thornycroft Shipbuilding)

better part of valour, Home's forces cut loose the captured E-Boat and beat a fighting retreat, managing to make good their escape whilst inflicting further damage on the attackers.

Meanwhile, the damaged S 111 was now taken under tow by its own side, and the return journey to Boulogne recommenced, with limited air cover from the Luftwaffe. No sooner had the Luftwaffe aircraft departed for home due to lack of fuel, than a formation of Spitfires arrived and attacked the German formation. After a battle between the E-Boats and the British aircraft had raged for half an hour, attempts to recover the ill-fated S 111 were abandoned and the vessel was cast adrift for the final time, this time to sink. Yet again, the superior speed, size and firepower of the German boats had been to some extent neutralized by the fearless determination of the commanders of the smaller British vessels.

On 16 April 1942, a major reorganization in the Kriegsmarine saw Rudolf Petersen, former commander of 2. S-Bootsflottille, promoted to the newly created position of Führer der Schnellboote, with the rank of Kapitän zur See, thus giving him command of all Germany's E-Boats. Operations continued. A mine-laying sortie on 18 April by four boats from 2. S-Bootsflottille and five from 4. S-Bootsflottille was responsible for seriously damaging two destroyers – HMS *Cotswold* and HMS *Quorn* – and sinking two merchants, *Plawsworth* and *Vae Vectis*. Three days later, however, E-Boats on their return to port were once again ambushed by boats from 6 MGB Flotilla. In the firefight that followed, S 52 was damaged and MGB 64 also suffered from several hits by German gunfire.

The Germans spent most of the remainder of the first half of 1942 on mine-laying operations, though on 12 May, 4. S-Bootsflottille was tasked with joining a large escort force, comprising 16 R-Boats and the torpedo boats *Seeadler*, *Kondor*, *Falke* and *Iltis*, to escort the auxiliary cruiser *Stier* through the Straits of Dover as she set out on a raiding mission. Before the E-Boats could take up position, however, the formation was attacked by MTBs, which had approached under the cover of a fog-bank. In the battle that ensued, MTB 220 was sunk and others damaged, but MTB 21 launched a torpedo at the *Stier* – the torpedo missed the cruiser, but hit the *Iltis*, breaking her back. Shortly afterwards, *Seeadler* was also hit by a torpedo, this time fired by MTB 221, and like her sister had her back broken. After the *Stier* was safely escorted into Boulogne, the E-Boats went out to sea again to pick up survivors, German and British, of the sunken ships.

ST NAZAIRE

One interesting use of an MTB, well beyond its normal duties, involved MTB 74. This Vosper-built boat had its torpedo tubes moved from the main deck up on to its raised forecastle. The repositioned tubes allowed them to be fired from a greater height and thus be able to clear the anti-torpedo nets protecting the German-occupied port of St Nazaire, when she took part in the famous raid alongside the destroyer HMS *Campbeltown*. On the night of the raid, 27/28 March 1942, and while under the command of Sub-Lieutenant R. Wynn, MTB 74 fired two 18in torpedoes – each packed with some 400kg of explosives – over the anti-torpedo nets, the torpedoes settling on the bottom just by the lock gates. The payload was detonated later by a delayed-action fuse, causing considerable damage. Sadly after this successful action MTB 74 then attempted to evacuate members of the destroyer's crew, and was hit by fire from German shore batteries. Only two of the crew survived the subsequent sinking, and were taken prisoner by the enemy. In total the raid on St Nazaire had cost British Coastal Forces one MTB, one MGB and 12 MLs.

The forward armament on a 70ft MTB, the twin 20mm Oerlikon. The boxes surrounding the position are ammunition lockers. (BAE Systems Surface Ships South, late Vosper Thornycroft Shipbuilding)

The summer months of 1942 once again saw night-time mine-laying sorties as the principal E-Boat operation, though a convoy attack on 8 July using the *Stichansatz* tactic by 2. S-Bootsflottille was highly effective, sinking six ships totalling around 12,000 tonnes. Convoy WP183 had been detected by the German radio monitoring service, and unknown to them E-Boats were closing in on their position. Torpedoes launched by S 67 hit the tanker *Pomella*, which rapidly sank. At the same time, S 48 sank the freighter *Kongshang*, S 109 sank the freighter *Rösten* and S 70 destroyed the small coaster *Boku*. The Dutch merchant *Reggestrom* was hit and sunk by a torpedo

MTB 74 is seen here prior to the raid on St Nazaire. Her torpedo tubes were moved up on to the forecastle to allow them to be fired over the top of the anti-torpedo nets in the German-occupied port. (BAE Systems Surface Ships South, late Vosper Thornycroft Shipbuilding)

RUDOLF PETERSEN

Rudolf Petersen was born on 15 June 1905 in Atzerballig in Denmark. He joined the Reichsmarine in 1925 and by the outbreak of war in 1939 had reached the rank of Kapitänleutnant and was in command of 2. Schnellbootsflottille. Petersen was promoted to Korvettenkapitän on 1 January 1940 and was awarded the Knight's Cross of the Iron Cross on 4 August of that year for his command of the flotilla during the campaign in the West. In November 1940 he was temporarily promoted to cover the post of Führer der Schnellboote (F.d.S., or Flag Officer E-Boats) and on 20 October 1941 was sent on staff officer training prior to him being elevated permanently to the post of F.d.S. in April 1942. He held this post throughout the remainder of the war, being promoted to Kapitän zur See on 1 April 1944. On 13 June 1944, Petersen was awarded the Oakleaves to his Knight's Cross in recognition of his achievements as F.d.S., and with the Oakleaves came the award of the special version of the E-Boat War Badge, with a diamond-encrusted swastika. Petersen died on 2 January 1983 in Flensburg, Schleswig-Holstein — he had been injured by fireworks thrown into his face on 31 December 1982, after opening his door to a group of teenagers celebrating the New Year.

Kapitän zur See Rudolf Petersen, Führer der Schnellboote. A highly experienced officer and one of only a small number of recipients of the rare E-Boat War Badge with Diamonds. (Author's collection)

from S 50. One of the escorts, the armed trawler *Manor*, was also hit and sunk, this time by a torpedo from S 63.

By contrast, a further convoy attack, made by a large force of some 19 E-Boats on 3 August 1942, was a total failure, without a single sinking being achieved. The tenacious defence of the convoy by its escorts, including a number of MGBs, saw off the German attackers.

DIEPPE

The next major operation to involve British coastal craft was the abortive landing at Dieppe on 19 August 1942. A number of MLs and MGBs were involved, as well as several ASRLs tasked with recovering the crews of any RAF aircraft shot down during the operation.

Although the operation itself ended in disaster, these small craft achieved some worthwhile successes. ML 346 attacked a small German tanker, the *Franz*, which was forced to ground herself on the shore. Incredibly, such was the ferocity of the attack that the survivors from the crew of the tanker reported having been attacked by a destroyer, and many of the crew simply jumped overboard. MLs 190 and 292 both shot down enemy aircraft, though this event may in fact have been a single 'shared' kill in the form of a Dornier Do 17 hit by fire from both vessels. Several other MLs, however, were damaged by fire from shore batteries and enemy aircraft.

In the autumn of 1942, a new German flotilla had arrived on the scene, 5. S-Bootsflottille under Kapitänleutnant Bernd Klug, and during this second half of the year operations by the E-Boats again achieved a good degree of success. This was partly due to the British transferring destroyers and other escort vessels, which would have protected British coastal convoys, to other duties, primarily escorting troopships heading towards North Africa. Four E-Boat flotillas were now available: 2. and 6. S-Bootsflottillen were at Ijmuiden, 4. S-Bootsflottille at Rotterdam and 5. S-Bootsflottille at Cherbourg.

On 10 September 1942, E-Boats were returning from a sortie in British waters when they were intercepted by four MGBs. One particular boat, MGB 335, was badly damaged and abandoned, and while the other E-Boats pursued the three remaining MGBs, sailors from S 80 and S 105 boarded the damaged British vessel. She was successfully towed into port, allowing the Germans to recover vital British charts plus radio and radar equipment. The boat was reported sunk by the Germans in an attempt to conceal the fact that this valuable material had been captured.

One interesting revelation from this incident was that one of the German boats, S 117, was equipped with the heavy 4cm gun and it was clear that projectiles from this weapon had pierced the armoured bridge of the British boat. As a result of this experience, recommendations were made regarding the increase in armour protection for the bridge area on E-Boats and for armament to be beefed up. Another large-scale convoy attack on 6 October 1942, by up to 17 E-Boats, sank three freighters, a tug and an ML.

British Coastal Forces scored a return victory on 14 October, when the auxiliary cruiser *Komet* was intercepted on her way out into the Atlantic on her second war cruise. The German raider was attacked by a number of British boats near Cap Le Hague and suffered direct hits by two torpedoes, launched from MTB 236. The raider, one of the smaller auxiliary cruisers, was literally blown apart. E-Boats from 5. S-Bootsflottille were ordered to recover survivors but could find none; all 274 of her crew were lost.

On 18 November, E-Boats had another successful night, when Convoy PW250 was attacked. An anti-submarine trawler, the

MTB 347 was part of an order for 16 boats placed with Vosper by the Royal Navy in April 1942. She was armed with two 21in torpedo tubes and a power-operated twin .5in machine-gun turret. (BAE Systems Surface Ships South, late Vosper Thornycroft Shipbuilding)

This view of the stern of MTB 347 affords a good view of the drum-like turret for the twin .5in machine guns, just aft of the wheelhouse. (BAE Systems Surface Ships South, late Vosper Thornycroft Shipbuilding)

MTB 355 shows the beefed-up armament fitted on many of the 70ft Vospers produced in 1942. The aft twin .5in machine guns have been replaced by a 20mm Oerlikon with a second Oerlikon mount fitted to the forecastle (the gun itself is not fitted in this shot). (BAE Systems Surface Ships South, late Vosper Thornycroft Shipbuilding)

Ullswater, and three merchantmen – the *Birgette*, the *Yew Forest* and the *Lab* – were sunk. The year also ended on a high note for the E-Boats. On 12 December, a feint attack by boats from 2. and 6. S-Bootsflottillen drew away the escorting warships from Convoy FN889, leaving it open to attack by boats from 4. S-Bootsflottille. They proceeded to sink five freighters: the *Avonwood*, the *Marianne*, the *Knitsley*, the *Lindisfarne* and the *Glentilt*. Despite the damage sustained by some of the E-Boats from gunfire from the escorts, this was a significant victory for Petersen's forces.

During 1942, E-Boats operating in the Channel had sunk two destroyers, one MGB, one ML, four armed trawlers and 19 merchants. In addition a further two destroyers and 19 other vessels had been sunk or damaged by mines laid by E-Boats. All in all, this represented a total of around 86,500 tonnes of shipping. By the end of the year, however, only around 16 E-Boats remained in a combat-ready condition, whilst opposing them were more than 130 MTBs and MGBs plus around 19 destroyers.

1943: THE TIDE TURNS

By 1943, the amount of British coastal convoy traffic had increased dramatically, offering many more targets for the E-Boats. Yet British escort forces had also been significantly increased, making it much more difficult for E-Boats to penetrate the protective screen around the convoys.

The new year would see some extremely audacious attacks by the E-Boats, with four E-Boats from 5. S-Bootsflottille charging into Lyme Bay on 20 February and launching torpedoes against ships that were assembling there for the formation of a convoy. A merchant ship, the *Moldavia*, and two armed auxiliaries – the whaler *Harstad* and the trawler *Lord Hailsham* – were sunk within a few minutes. A Landing Craft, Tank – LCT 381 – was also boarded and her crew taken prisoner before the ship was torpedoed and sunk. The E-Boats then sped off again, having achieved several sinkings and taken a number of prisoners.

German sorties under the cover of darkness continued, despite the growing strength of British escort forces, not only in the form of frigates and destroyers but also heavily armed Beaufighter, Typhoon and Spitfire aircraft, which made daylight operations perilous. The British Coastal Forces, however, were under no similar limitations, as virtually no Luftwaffe forces were available to support E-Boat operations in daylight.

On 4 March, Petersen despatched his E-Boats to make an attack on a southbound convoy that had been detected leaving Scottish waters. Unfortunately for the German force, S 70 ran on to a mine and sank. The remainder of the 2. S-Bootsflottille boats picked up the survivors and headed back to port, while the E-Boats from the other flotillas continued with their mission. The British had detected the German movements, however. Two destroyers, HMS *Windsor* and HMS *Southdown*, along with the corvette HMS *Sheldrake* were waiting for the E-Boats off Lowestoft and drove them back. Giving up any further attempts to intercept the convoy, the E-Boats headed for home, but on the way S 74 and S 75 were attacked by British fighters and S 74 was sunk. The whole operation had been a disaster for Petersen, but an encouraging victory for British Coastal Forces.

On 7 March 1943, the tables were again turned on the Germans, when S 114 and S 119 came under attack by the elderly *Campbell*-class destroyer HMS *Mackey*, supported by MTB 20 and MTB 21. Turning tail and withdrawing at top speed, the two E-Boats crashed into each other, with S 119 being left a complete write-off. Her crew were taken onboard by S 114, which eventually reached her home base safely.

On 28 March, MGBs 321 and 323 intercepted boats from 2. S-Bootsflottille which were en route to attack Convoy FS1074. The heavily armed MGBs inflicted severe damage on S 29, first with gunfire from their 4cm guns, then by ramming. Although her crew was recovered by other E-Boats, S 29 was so badly damaged that she had to be scuttled.

On the night of 13 April, four E-Boats from 5. S-Bootsflottille attacked a convoy of 22 ships, PW323, off the coast of Cornwall. Many of the torpedoes launched by the E-Boats missed their targets, but S 121 scored a hit on the freighter *Stanlake* whilst a combined attack by S 65, S 90 and S 112 saw three torpedo hits on the destroyer HNMS *Eskdale*, which quickly capsized and sank. The E-Boats then escaped unharmed.

The midsummer months for the E-Boats were taken up with high-speed mine-laying operations in the narrow waters of the Channel, longer-range missions now being particularly hazardous due to difficulties in reaching and returning from the operational areas, all under the cover of darkness during the short summer nights.

The MGBs, meanwhile, continued to lurk along the anticipated routes taken by the E-Boats in the hope of intercepting them during their return to base. On 24 July, MGBs once again came off best against E-Boats, when S 77 was lost during an engagement. One of her torpedoes was hit by enemy gunfire and detonated, causing the boat to sink.

By the time the summer months were over, most of the E-Boats operating in the Channel had been retrofitted with the new armoured bridge, offering far better protection to

An E-Boat draws up alongside a pier in port. Notable here are the canvas 'dodgers' hung over the ship's railings to give the crew some measure of protection from spray, a luxury not afforded to the crews of British boats. (Hermann Büchting via R. Mills)

Korvettenkapitän Felix Zymalkowski commanded 8. S-Bootsflottille. By the time he earned his Knight's Cross in April 1945, he had undertaken 139 combat missions. (Author's collection)

the commander and his bridge crew. On 12 September, 8. S-Bootsflottille arrived in Rotterdam.

A major engagement between the small coastal craft of both sides occurred on the night of 24/25 September. Boats from all of the E-Boat flotillas were in action on that night, but minor problems hit Petersen's forces from the start. S 87 had to withdraw with engine problems and S 74 and S 90 collided with each other, forcing them both to return to base.

Three other E-Boats – S 86, S 96 and S 99 – encountered four British armed trawlers: the *Stella Leonis*, *Stella Rigel*, *Donna Nook* and *Franc Tireur*, which together formed part of a convoy escort. The latter was almost immediately struck by a torpedo launched by S 96, giving first blood to the E-Boats. Reinforcements in the shape of ML 145 and ML 150 then arrived for the British warships, with ML 145 ramming S 96 so hard that the two vessels locked together. The Germans managed to disengage from the British launch, but as she did so ML 150 arrived on the spot and the opposing crews began pouring fire on each other. Outnumbered, the Germans were forced to scuttle their boat, the crew survivors being picked up by the British. Both the MLs, however, suffered severe damage.

As this engagement indicates, by now the E-Boats were facing extremely difficult conditions, with British escort forces at their strongest. It has been estimated that, as well as destroyers and corvettes, more than 100 MGBs and MLs were available for convoy protection duty.

A night attack on a convoy on 24 October 1943, involving a large force of 31 E-Boats, this time under the personal leadership of Kapitän zur See Petersen, resulted in similar disaster. Two boats from 4. S-Bootsflottille – S 63 and S 88 – were sunk and the flotilla commander, Korvettenkapitän Werner Lützow, older brother of the famous fighter ace Günther Lützow, was killed.

The events of the night played out as follows. That evening, a coastal convoy with a heavy escort of destroyers was sailing northbound towards the River Humber with a number of MGBs and MLs, not specifically assigned to the convoy but on patrol in the vicinity. Late in the evening, one of the escort destroyers, HMS *Pytchley*, detected the approaching E-Boats by radar and drove them off with accurate gunfire, seriously damaging at least one of them. The MGBs in the area were then directed to intercept the E-Boats on their return leg. The large formation of E-Boats had split into smaller groups and were then involved in running battles with destroyer escorts as they attempted, in vain, to reach the convoy, though the straggling trawler *William Stephen* was caught by the E-Boats and sunk.

The E-Boats then made their way home, travelling at low speed because one of their number, S 63, had been damaged earlier by gunfire from the destroyer HMS *Mackay*. The MGBs that had been waiting to intercept them made contact in the early hours of the morning, and attacked immediately with all guns blazing. The limping S 63 was an obvious target, and when S 88 attempted to come to her aid, she was attacked by two MGBs – 607 and 610 – suffering severe damage, and was soon ablaze. The MGBs then turned their attention back to the damaged S 63, and MGB 607 rammed her, causing her to sink though damaging herself in the process. As MGB 610 came to the assistance of her fellow gun boat, the nearby S 88 exploded. The convoy defences had been just too strong for the E-Boats and the only sinking was the small trawler, which was a straggler rather than in convoy.

This view of MTB 381 gives a good impression of the amount of spray that was thrown up by boats at high speed and why they would normally approach an enemy under cover of darkness at low speed to avoid the spray alerting the enemy. (BAE Systems Surface Ships South, late Vosper Thornycroft Shipbuilding)

With the E-Boats, as with so many other parts of the German military machine, replacement vessels were becoming harder to produce as the tides of war turned against the Third Reich. Not only were the boats themselves precious, but the loss of trained crews was becoming harder to sustain.

The 5. S-Bootsflottille, meanwhile, had been somewhat more successful, and on 2 November nine boats from the flotilla attacked a convoy off Dungeness, sinking three merchant ships. The target this time was Convoy CW221, which had initially been detected by Luftwaffe reconnaissance aircraft. E-Boats raced to intercept the convoy and after some initial manoeuvring to get into a good attack position, S 100 torpedoed and sank the small steamer *Foam Queen*, whilst S 138 sank the coaster *Storia* and S 136 scored a hit on and sank the freighter *Dona Isabel*. Although the total tonnage sunk was modest, what marked this operation as particularly successful was that the convoy escorts seemed helpless to prevent the attack, which was carried out at high speed.

During 1943, some 26 ships representing just under 45,000 tonnes had been sunk by E-Boats, a much lower figure than the previous year and an indication of the much greater strength of British convoy defence measures. As victory totals had dropped, so had E-Boat losses increased, with 12 boats lost in the second half of the year alone.

1944: DEFEAT FOR THE E-BOATS

The opening days of 1944 saw another audacious attack by E-Boats from 5. S-Bootsflottille. WP457, a convoy escorted by two destroyers and four armed trawlers, in transit off the coast of Cornwall, was attacked by seven E-Boats on 5 January. The attackers launched salvoes of torpedoes directly at the escorts. This opening tactic forced the escorts into making violent evasive manoeuvres, leaving gaps in the escort screen through which the E-Boats roared, launching a second salvo against the freighters. Three merchant ships, the *Polperro*, the *Underwood* and the *Solstad* (an armed trawler) were sunk before the E-Boats sped off without loss.

The 5. S-Bootsflottille enjoyed a further success at the end of January, when seven boats from the flotilla detected Convoy CW243 by radar and were able to launch a surprise attack on the British. Whilst five of the E-Boats distracted the relatively heavy escort, which comprised two destroyers, three armed trawlers and six MLs, S 138 and S 142 roared out of the darkness and attacked the tail-end of the convoy. The trawler *Pine* was hit by a torpedo from S 142, and shortly afterwards the small coastal freighter *Emerald* was hit by another torpedo from the same E-Boat. Meanwhile S 138 had torpedoed and sunk the freighter *Caleb Sprague*.

For the E-Boats, February 1944 was primarily taken up with mine-laying operations, with no particularly significant engagements apart from the sinking of the armed trawler *Cap d'Antifer* in the mouth of the Humber by S 65 and S99 on 13 February.

Around that same time, 9. S-Bootsflottille was moved into Cherbourg, increasing the forces available to Petersen, though the additional resources did not lead to any great improvement in tallies for the E-Boats.

Operations were becoming increasingly difficult and dangerous as the Allies began the massive build-up of resources in the south-east of England, in preparation for the eventual invasion of occupied France in the summer of that year.

EXERCISE *TIGER*

One major episode in which E-Boats and MTBs were involved was the tragedy that occurred at Slapton Sands in the spring of 1944. In the run-up to the Allied invasion of Normandy, the south of England was awash with troops preparing for the momentous battle. Training exercises were an important part of honing the abilities of both the naval and army elements that were about to take part in the landings. One such training exercise was code-named Exercise *Tiger*, and involved the landing of some 30,000 troops with armour support on the beach at Slapton Sands.

In the early hours of 28 April, a flotilla of eight Landing Ship, Tank (LST) vessels carrying a large number of tanks and thousands of troops was approaching the designated area under the cover of darkness. Escort support was provided by the Royal Navy in the form of a corvette, HMS *Azelea*, and an outer defensive screen of three MTBs and two MGBs. As the convoy approached its destination in line astern formation (thus offering a wide target area to the enemy), six E-Boats from 5. S-Bootsflottille, based in Cherbourg, slipped through the MTB/MGB screen and came roaring out of the darkness.

The six boats split into three *Rotten* of two boats each, and attacked with the advantage of total surprise. It is believed that the *Rotte* comprising S 136 and S 138 was responsible for torpedo strikes on LST 507 and LST 531. A second *Rotte* consisting of S 140 and S 142 failed to achieve any hits, but the third – S 100 and S 143 – achieved at least one hit, probably on LST 289. LST 507 caught fire and was soon blazing fiercely. It had to be abandoned by its crew, with more than 200 occupants lost. LST 531 began to sink, and within just seven minutes of the ship being hit, the survivors had abandoned the stricken vessel. It soon slipped beneath the waves, taking with it 424 crew members and troops. The third damaged LST also caught fire, but despite the damage eventually made it to safety. Three further E-Boats – S 130, S 145 and S 150, all from 9. Schnellbootsflottille (also based in Cherbourg) – now arrived on the scene, but although they engaged the enemy, no further serious losses were inflicted.

Now taking heavy defensive fire from the escorts and other LSTs, the E-Boats made good their escape. The fatalities suffered by the Allies were horrendous. In fact, more lives were lost in this exercise than on the actual invasion landings on Utah Beach on D-Day. To make matters worse, it is thought that many of those US troops who reached the beaches were killed by 'friendly fire', having ended up outside of the designated safe area. Furthermore, several of those lost were carrying details of the actual invasion plans, and the authorities had no way of knowing if the planning materials had been recovered by the Germans. Fortunately for the Allies, the bodies of the relevant individuals were all later recovered.

A particularly sad occasion for the Kriegsmarine occurred on 13 May 1944. Klaus Dönitz, the elder son of the commander-in-chief of the Navy, Grossadmiral Karl Dönitz, had been in service in U-Boats. Yet as the sole surviving son after his brother Peter, also in U-Boats, was lost at sea with U 954 on 19 May 1943, Klaus was transferred to shore duty and began training as a naval doctor. He maintained contact with many of his former comrades, however, and to celebrate his birthday on 13 May 1944, persuaded some of his friends in the S-Bootwaffe to take him along as an observer on an operational sortie on S 141.

Whilst in waters off the Solent, the E-Boat was detected by radar by the French destroyer *La Combattante*, which opened fire. S 141 was hit near the stern and set on fire. Attempts by other E-Boats to distract the destroyer were to no avail, and the French warship approached to virtually point-blank range and poured fire on the hapless E-Boat. Klaus Dönitz, who should have been serving ashore on non-combatant duties, was one of those killed.

Once the Allied invasion of Normandy began, the sheer volume of escort forces protecting the sea routes between England and France, combined with heavy bombing raids on the E-Boat bases, made E-Boat operations extremely difficult. On the day of the invasion, there were five flotillas based on the Channel coast: 5. and 9. S-Bootsflottillen at Cherbourg; 4. S-Bootsflottille at Boulogne; 2. S-Bootsflottille at Ostend and 8. S-Bootsflottille at Ijmuiden. Of these, the two Cherbourg units were sent out on patrol, but encountered no enemy shipping. However, 5. S-Bootsflottille ran into the defensive destroyer screen protecting the Allied convoy lanes and managed to sink the Norwegian destroyer *Svenner*.

Boats from 4. S-Bootsflottille, now under the command of Korvettenkapitän Kurt Fimmen, also attempted to intervene on 6 June, but almost immediately on leaving port they were attacked by the O-class destroyer HMS *Obedient* and a swarm of MTBs, and were forced to return to base. Over the coming days, E-Boats and R-Boats made determined attempts to penetrate the screens of MTBs and MGBs protecting the flanks of the Allied invasion convoys, but without any significant

OVERLEAF

As part of the preparations for the D-Day landings, early on the morning of 28 April 1944 a convoy of fully laden LSTs was heading for the beach at Slapton Sands in Devon to practise landing operations. The convoy was protected by destroyers, MTBs and MGBs, but this protective screen was infiltrated by a number of E-Boats, which attacked the convoy, making torpedo strikes on three of the LSTs. One was so badly damaged that it was abandoned while the second was heavily damaged but made it safely back to port; the third, LST 531, sank rapidly after being hit, with heavy loss of life. Ironically, more men were lost during this disaster – over 600 – than the 200 who were lost during the real landing at Utah Beach for which this was the practice. The tragedy was made all the worse by even more lives being lost to 'friendly fire', when troops landing on the beach wandered into an area that was being subjected to live firing.

Our plate shows a torpedo strike on LST 531 by an unidentified E-Boat from 9. Schnellbootsflottille, based in Cherbourg. Boats from both 5. and 9. Schnellbootsflottillen were involved in the attack. The actual boat that fired the fatal torpedo at LST 531 has not been positively identified. It may well have been S 130, which survived the war and is now undergoing restoration in the UK.

Kapitänleutnant Kurt Fimmen, captain of S 19 and S 26 before becoming commander of 4. S-Bootsflottille. Note the E-Boat War Badge worn just under his Iron Cross. (Author's collection)

success. Several British boats were badly damaged in these engagements, however.

As we know, Hitler at first believed that the Normandy landings were merely a feint, with the real invasion to come at the Pas de Calais. For that reason, defensive forces that may have resisted the landings were held in reserve, awaiting landings that never came. For the same reason, only 5. and 9. S-Bootsflottillen were allocated to attack the Normandy landing forces, with 2., 4. and 8. S-Bootsflottillen held back to patrol the coast further north.

Boats from 5. and 9. S-Bootsflottillen did indeed intercept traffic on their way to the invasion beaches, but failed to score any hits with the torpedoes they launched. This failure was made worse by the loss of two boats – S 139 and S 140 – both of which ran onto mines on the return voyage to their base. Eventually, 2. and 4. S-Bootsflottillen were also allocated for attacks against the invasion forces. On 8 June, boats from 9. S-Bootsflottille penetrated the defence screens and sank two landing craft, whilst those from 5. S-Bootsflottille launched torpedoes at a number of warships, scoring a hit on and damaging the destroyer USS *Meredith*. The warship was finished off by a Luftwaffe bomber the following morning.

On 10 June, the same two flotillas once again penetrated the Allied defences and sank several vessels, including two tugs and an MTB, with a destroyer and a landing ship damaged. Boats from 2. and 4. S-Bootsflottillen sank three vessels, including an ammunition ship, and also sowed mines in the Allied shipping lanes. The following day, two boats from 5. and 9. S-Bootsflottillen – S 84 and S 100 – engaged and crippled the British MTB 448 (which later sank as a result of shelling from MTB 453), though S 136 was later intercepted by a group of Allied warships and was herself sunk.

The sheer number of Allied warships, to say nothing of overwhelming air power, now operating in the Channel area was making resupply very difficult for the E-Boat flotillas, some of which were running low on torpedoes. The sinking of an MTB or E-Boat by enemy aircraft was a relatively rare event, but the RAF achieved a significant victory on 13 June when heavy, two-engined Beaufighters attacked and sank three E-Boats and one R-Boat in a single engagement. Unbeknown to the Germans, an even greater disaster was looming as the British determined to try to eliminate the threat of Petersen's E-Boat forces.

The E-Boats were operating out of Le Havre, owing to its good location for attacks against the invasion beaches, but this was not a formal E-Boat base and had no protective bunkers. Nor did it have a torpedo arsenal, and was one of the bases worst hit by supply shortages. Nevertheless, a large-scale attack was planned against the invasion forces, and in view of this 5. and 9. S-Bootsflottillen were ordered to return to Cherbourg, from where an attack would be launched against the western flank of the Allied lines. Unfortunately, not long after leaving port, a major storm forced the E-Boats to return to the shelter of Le Havre. The British, however, had intercepted German radio signals referring to this occurrence, and ordered an immediate bombing raid.

Doubly unfortunate for the Germans was the fact that because of expected Luftwaffe activity over the port on that night, Flak defences had been warned not to open fire, so when a formation of Lancaster bombers appeared over Le Havre they were unopposed. A total of 15 E-Boats were tied up in Le Havre when the raid took place on 14 June, and of that total only one, S 167, escaped total destruction. To make matters worse, many other craft, including three torpedo boats, eight minesweepers and eight VP-Boats were also destroyed. A second air assault the following night against Boulogne also caused a significant loss of warships for the Kriegsmarine, but fortunately for Petersen, his E-Boats had departed their bunkers and were unharmed. Nevertheless, his total forces in the area had been slashed by more than half.

Now 2. and 4. S-Bootsflottillen were merged and sent into action almost immediately. Cherbourg itself was under threat of capture, and with Boulogne likely to see further Allied air attacks, the remaining E-Boats were now to operate out of Le Havre and Dieppe. For a short period, a new type of pressure mine available to the E-Boats allowed them to regain some measure of success, but the capture of an example of the new mine by the Allies allowed them to introduce effective countermeasures, so the upturn was very short lived.

Reinforcements eventually arrived in the form of 6. and 10. S-Bootsflottillen, which had been transferred westwards from the Baltic. On 27 July 1944, five boats from 2. S-Bootsflottille in Le Havre set out to attack enemy shipping and soon ran into a number of MTBs. The engagement that ensued took place at close quarters, and during the fierce battle MTB 430 was rammed by one of the E-Boats, S 182. Shortly thereafter, MTB 412 collided with the wreck of her fellow MTB and all three boats sank. The remaining four E-Boats hastily withdrew.

On 30 July, eight boats from 6. S-Bootsflottille succeeded in penetrating the relatively heavy escort screen around Convoy FTM53 off Dungeness and between them launched six torpedoes, of which five hit their targets. The freighter *Samwake* was sunk and four others – the *Fort Dearborne*, *Fort Kaskaskia*, *Ocean Volga* and *Ocean Courier* – were damaged. Despite being fast and relatively well armed, both E-Boats and their British counterparts were highly susceptible to enemy fire and needed to use their speed and agility to avoid being hit.

An E-Boat crewman at the hydraulic controls used to fire the torpedo from its tube. The leather jacket was typical working dress for E-Boat crewmen. (Hermann Büchting via R. Mills)

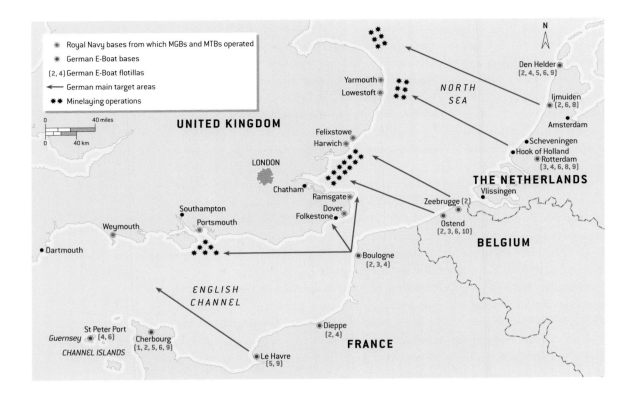

Royal Navy bases from which MGBs and MTBs operated
German E-Boat bases
(2, 4) German E-Boat flotillas
German main target areas
✱✱ Minelaying operations

This map shows the disposition of E-Boat forces just before the Allied invasion of France in the summer of 1944. The numbers next to each base indicate the flotillas that operated from these bases. It can be seen that the E-Boat flotillas, or parts of the flotillas, moved around quite frequently. The red arrows indicate the principal target areas of operations launched from these ports, with the clusters of black dots indicating areas where E-Boats were heavily involved in mine-laying operations.

As the Allied invasion of France progressed, fewer and fewer ports were available to the Germans, though bases in the Channel Islands at the extreme south of the map and occupied Holland in the north remained available for operations until the very last stages of the war.

Petersen now turned his attention away from attacking the invasion fleet and back to striking against coastal convoys, where there was a greater chance of success, not only in the possibility of sinking merchants, but in tying down more warships as escorts. On 30 July, a modest victory was achieved when three boats from 6. S-Bootsflottille – S 91, S 97 and S 114 – attacked a convoy, sinking a freighter as well as seriously damaging four other supply ships before escaping unscathed, no mean feat at this point in the war. Unfortunately for Petersen, the British took their revenge over the next few days with bombing raids on Le Havre that destroyed two boats (S 39 and S 114) and damaged five others.

The invasion of Normandy in June 1944 presented the Germans with considerable problems in maintaining supplies for their garrisons on the occupied Channel Islands. Here, boats from 65 (Canadian) MTB Flotilla based in Plymouth intercepted a German convoy on the night of 3 July, sank two merchants and damaged a third.

The newly formed 10. S-Bootsflottille arrived in the Channel on 7 August with six fresh boats. Although it carried out mine-laying operations in the Thames Estuary, no Allied ships were sunk. Unfortunately for the Germans, intercepts of their radio traffic by the British allowed the mined areas to be identified quickly, and shipping traffic was diverted until they were cleared. On 9 August, however, the cruiser HMS *Frobisher* and the minesweeper HMS *Vestal* were hit by torpedoes fired from E-Boats. The cruiser suffered sufficient damage that she was disarmed and downgraded to use as a cadet training ship. Though the minesweeper survived this attack, she would subsequently serve in the Far East and be hit and sunk by a Japanese *kamikaze* aircraft in July 1945.

On 10 August, a large freighter, the *Iddesleigh*, and a repair ship, HMS *Albatross*, were also hit by E-Boat torpedoes. Time, however, was running out for Petersen's forces in occupied France and Belgium. On 29 August, his boats finally pulled out of Le Havre and on 4 September Boulogne too was abandoned. Even after the recent reinforcements, the E-Boat force available for operations in the Channel was a mere 33 boats, faced by at least 160 of their opposite numbers on the British side. Despite this, Petersen's E-Boats were still managing to mount occasional successful strikes against British coastal convoys, using both torpedoes and mines, and often doing so without losses on their own side.

Mining operations brought worthwhile results for the Germans in November when, on the fifth of the month, LCT 457 hit a mine laid by E-Boats and capsized. Just two days later, LCT 976 and LST 420 hit mines laid during the same operation and were also sunk. British aircraft launched a further heavy bombing raid on the E-Boat bases, hitting Ijmuiden on 15 December and causing serious damage, but the Allies' attention was diverted from the threat posed by the E-Boats when, on 16 December, Hitler launched his last major offensive in the West, pouring troops and tanks into the Ardennes.

The E-Boats would now be tasked with hitting Allied supply routes into the port of Antwerp. In the event, promised reinforcements in the form of 2., 4., 5. and 6. S-Bootsflottillen would not appear in time to have an effect on the military situation. Any hope of the E-Boats having a major impact against Allied supply convoys was ruled out when Grossadmiral Dönitz refused permission for Petersen's E-Boats to carry out what might have been effective mine-laying operations, as he wished to keep the waters clear for the possible use of *Seehund* midget submarines. The year ended badly for Petersen when, on 23 December, S 185 and S 192 were caught and sunk by British warships. Attempts by other E-Boats to come to their aid were prevented by British escort warships.

A typical 73ft MTB with full armament. Note that as well as the twin Oerlikon, twin .303in Lewis machine guns are attached to the forward torpedo tubes and twin .5in Vickers machine guns to the aft tubes. (BAE Systems Surface Ships South, late Vosper Thornycroft Shipbuilding)

1945: FINAL ACTIONS

The final year of the war opened with Petersen's forces numbering just 26 boats, spread over five flotillas. With the final arrival of the promised reinforcements, Petersen now had 2. S-Bootsflottille at Den Helder, 4., 6. and 9. S-Bootsflottillen at Rotterdam and 8. S-Bootsflottille at Ijmuiden. Further reinforcements in the form of 5. S-Bootsflottille arrived at Den Helder on 13 January, with eight additional boats.

Several operations were launched in the second half of January, but successes were meagre, with a few merchants damaged and one freighter and one LST sunk. The E-Boats, on the other hand, lost two of their own number sunk and several damaged.

During February, permission was given for mine-laying sorties in the areas previously designated for *Seehund* operations. A mine-laying mission on 17 February resulted in the sinking of the French destroyer *La Combattante* and the trawler *Aquarius*, as well as two freighters damaged.

Some modest victories were scored against coastal convoys, but arguments over tactics still raged between Petersen as commander of the E-Boats and Dönitz as commander-in-chief of the Kriegsmarine. Dönitz was still intent on applying severe restrictions to the areas in the Scheldt estuary in which the E-Boats were permitted to carry out mine-laying missions. The level of success that Petersen might have achieved, had he been allowed freedom of action, may be judged from the fact that in just one week following one of his mine-laying operations, 25,000 tonnes of shipping was sunk by E-Boat-deployed mines.

Towards the end of January 1945, further attempts were made to intercept British convoys. On the night of 22 January, a total of 16 boats from 4., 6., 8. and 9. S-Bootsflottillen set off to intercept Allied shipping. Facing them on convoy escort duty were a frigate, a sloop and 44 MTBs. Boats from 6. and 8. S-Bootsflottillen were

A fine study of the Vosper Type II 73ft MTB ordered for the Royal Navy in 1945. The number of torpedo tubes has once again been reduced to two, principally because the lack of targets by now available meant a heavy torpedo load was pointless. The forward weapon is now the 6pdr quick-firing (QF) gun. (BAE Systems Surface Ships South, late Vosper Thornycroft Shipbuilding)

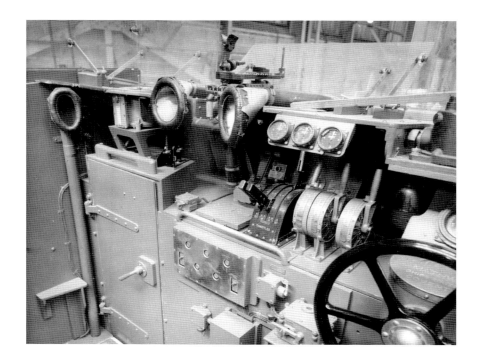

Although slightly more spacious than previous versions, the wheelhouse of a 73ft Vosper Type II as shown here was still narrower and more cramped than that of its German counterpart. (BAE Systems Surface Ships South, late Vosper Thornycroft Shipbuilding)

unable to penetrate the protective screen of enemy warships, but S 168 and S 175 from 9. S-Bootsflottille succeeded in launching torpedoes, which hit and sank the freighter *Halo*. Response from the escorts was swift and S 168 suffered heavy damage before being able to escape.

Boats from 8. S-Bootsflottille also launched multiple torpedoes at a convoy in the Thames Estuary, all of which missed their targets. The escorting destroyers and MTBs reacted with such ferocity that the E-Boats were forced to beat a hasty retreat, and in the process S 199 and S 701 collided. S 199 had to be abandoned and was later destroyed by coastal artillery fire.

Operations were becoming ever more difficult with the sheer strength of Allied escort forces, both warships and aircraft, making successful attacks almost impossible. On 22 February, however, a force of 22 E-Boats set off to hunt for convoys in British coastal waters. Boats from 2. and 5. S-Bootsflottillen intercepted a convoy near Great Yarmouth and sank the freighters *Goodwood* and *Blacktoft* and seriously damaged a third, the *Skjold*. At the same time, boats from 8. S-Bootsflottille intercepted shipping in the Thames Estuary and sank a landing craft, though not without some cost, as S 193 was destroyed by fire from the British escorts.

A night attack on 28 February/1 March by boats from 2., 4., 5. and 6. S-Bootsflottillen achieved little other than a few mines being laid, the E-Boats being driven off by powerful escort forces with one boat (S 220) sunk and several others damaged. A further operation on 12 March by 2., 4., 6. and 9. S-Bootsflottillen was slightly more successful, with the E-Boats penetrating the escort screens and laying more than 120 mines, as well as sinking two merchant ships. On the following day, a further large-scale mine-laying sortie was carried out, involving all the E-Boat

Looking towards the bridge and wheelhouse of a Vosper Type II, with the breech end of the 6pdr quick-firing gun to the right. The end of the war meant that only a small number of this type were built in 1945 before production ceased. (BAE Systems Surface Ships South, late Vosper Thornycroft Shipbuilding)

flotillas, with a total force of 25 boats. Although boats from 2., 5. and 9. S-Bootsflottillen were driven off by the escorts, others from 4. and 6. S-Bootsflottillen succeeded in sinking two transport ships, the *Samselbu* and the *Empire Blessing*. A week later, the landing ship LST 80, the Liberty Ships *Hadley F Brown* and *Charles D MacIver*, the freighter *Eleftheria* and the Motor Launch ML 466 were all lost to mines laid by the E-Boats. Even though several E-Boats were damaged in battles with MGBs during these operations, it is clear that determined operations by the E-Boats, even at this late stage of the war, were capable of causing painful losses to the Allies.

The remaining weeks of the war saw no major E-Boat successes against British convoys, as German fuel supplies ran drastically low. Despite the difficulties faced by Petersen's forces in 1945, the E-Boats had still managed to sink 31 enemy ships representing around 89,000 tonnes of enemy shipping through a combination of torpedoes and mines, as well as damaging a further seven enemy ships of around 26,500 tonnes.

The last days of fighting, however, did see another example of determined action by the smaller British craft against a larger German formation. On the night of 6/7 April, E-Boats unsuccessfully attempted an attack on a British convoy, before laying mines and heading for home. They were detected by aircraft from RAF Coastal Command, which guided a formation of MTBs from 22 MTB Flotilla to intercept them. The MTBs burst into the centre of the German formation with all guns blazing. One British boat, MTB 494, sank after a collision with S 176, which also sank. S 177 was so seriously damaged that it had to be abandoned, whilst MTB 493, though seriously damaged, was towed safely back to port in Lowestoft. Yet more misfortune struck the E-Boats on the following day, when 4. and 6. S-Bootsflottillen were both engaged by British warships, including the frigate HMS *Rutherford* and MTBs 482 and 454. In the pell-mell action that ensued, S 202 and S 703 sank after colliding and S 223 went down after hitting a mine.

MTBs were also involved in what would be the last action of the war for the E-Boats. On 14 April, MTBs 746 and 797, in conjunction with the frigate HMS *Ekins*, intercepted 12 boats from 4. and 9. S-Bootsflottillen, which were on a mine-laying sortie. In the firefight which followed, S 205 was badly damaged, as were the two MTBs, though the damage suffered by these smaller boats was less serious. The E-Boats did, however, succeed in laying a number of mines that would be responsible for the sinking of the small tanker *Gold Shell* as well as damaging the *Conakrian,* and the Liberty Ships *Benjamin H Bristow* and *Horace Binney*.

STATISTICAL ANALYSIS

BRITISH LOSSES

MTB/MGB/ML losses, 1940–45						
	1940	1941	1942	1943	1944	1945
Jan			1	1		
Feb		1		1	1	14
Mar			13	1	3	1
Apr					1	2
May		1	1	1	2	1
Jun		2	2	2	5	
Jul		2	4	1	6	
Aug	1		5	1	3	
Sep	1	1	2	1	1	
Oct	4		3	1	3	
Nov	2			3	1	
Dec	2		1		1	
Totals	10	7	32	13	27	18

As British coastal craft often ended up in a confusing melee with combined German forces comprising E-Boats, R-Boats and torpedo boats, it was not always possible to determine with absolute certainty which German craft would have fired the shots that destroyed the British craft. In many cases, it is only possible to determine whether the German vessel involved was either an E-Boat or some other surface craft.

MTB/MGB/ML LOSSES BY TYPE, 1940–45:

MTB losses, 1940–45						
	1940	**1941**	**1942**	**1943**	**1944**	**1945**
Jan			1	1		
Feb		1				13
Mar			1	1	3	
Apr					1	2
May			1		2	
Jun			1		4	
Jul					6	
Aug			4		1	
Sep	1					
Oct	3		2	1	2	
Nov				3		
Dec			1		1	
Totals	4	1	11	6	20	15

MTBs SUNK IN DIRECT ACTION AGAINST E-BOATS:

MTB 29 sunk after collision with E-Boat, 6 October 1942
MTB 220 sunk in battle with a number of E-Boats from 4. and 5. S-Bootsflottillen, 13 May 1942
MTB 430 sunk after ramming by E-Boat S 182, 26 July 1944
MTB 494 sunk after collision with E-Boat S 176, 7 April 1945
MTB 5001 sunk by E-Boats S 209 and 210, 7 April 1945

MTBs SUNK BY OTHER SURFACE VESSELS:

MTB 43 sunk by German surface craft, 18 August 1942
MTB 44 sunk by German surface craft, 7 August 1942
MTB 47 sunk by German surface craft, 17 January 1942

MTB 201 sunk by German surface craft, 15 June 1942
MTB 218 sunk by German surface craft, 18 August 1942
MTB 237 sunk by German surface craft, 7 August 1942
MTB 241 sunk by German surface craft, 31 March 1944
MTB 347 sunk by German surface craft, 1 October 1944
MTB 356 sunk by German surface craft, 16 October 1943
MTB 360 sunk by German surface craft, 1 October 1944
MTB 417 sunk by German surface craft, 15 March 1944
MTB 434 sunk by German surface craft, 9 July 1944
MTB 606 sunk by German surface craft, 3 November 1943
MTB 622 sunk by German surface craft, 10 March 1943
MTB 666 sunk by German surface craft, 4 July 1944
MTB 681 sunk by German surface craft, 9 June 1944

MGB losses, 1940–45						
	1940	1941	1942	1943	1944	1945
Jan						
Feb				1		
Mar						
Apr						
May		1		1		1
Jun		2	1	2	1	
Jul		2	4	1		
Aug	1			1	1	
Sep			1			
Oct			1		1	
Nov						
Dec	2					
Totals	3	5	7	6	3	1

MGBs SUNK IN DIRECT ACTION AGAINST E-BOATS:

MGB 76 sunk by E-Boat, 6 October 1942

MGBs SUNK BY OTHER SURFACE VESSELS:

MGB 18 sunk by German surface craft, 30 September 1942
MGB 78 sunk by German surface craft, 2 October 1942

MGB 79 sunk by German surface craft, 28 February 1943
MGB 110 sunk by German surface craft, 29 May 1943
MGB 601 sunk by German surface craft, 24 July 1943

ML losses, 1940–45						
	1940	**1941**	**1942**	**1943**	**1944**	**1945**
Jan						
Feb					1	1
Mar			12			1
Apr						
May						
Jun						
Jul						
Aug			1		1	
Sep		1		1	1	
Oct	1		1			
Nov	2				1	
Dec						
Totals	3	1	14	1	4	2

GERMAN LOSSES

E-Boat losses, 1940–45						
	1940	**1941**	**1942**	**1943**	**1944**	**1945**
Jan				1		2
Feb			1	1	2	2
Mar		1	1	3	2	7
Apr						4
May					2	3
Jun	1	2			20	
Jul	1			4	2	
Aug	1			1	11	
Sep				2	4	

E-Boat losses, 1940–45 (cont.)

	1940	1941	1942	1943	1944	1945
Oct	1			2		
Nov	1	1		3		
Dec			1		3	
Totals	5	4	3	17	46	18

These figures do not include losses in areas such as Norway, the Mediterranean, the Black Sea, etc., only those relevant to the area around the English Channel. A significant number of E-Boats were lost not to action with enemy MTBs or larger warships, but to air attack, either at sea or, more frequently as the war progressed, by bombing attacks on their bases. Although E-Boats occasionally utilized the same massive bunkers used by the U-Boats, they were often moored in the open, making inviting targets for Allied aircraft. In a single raid on the harbour at Le Havre on the night of 14 June 1944, RAF bombers destroyed a total of three torpedo boats, 14 E-Boats and two R-Boats.

MTB 33 was bombed and damaged by the Luftwaffe while still under construction in Portsmouth, showing that it was not only the E-Boats that suffered from aerial attack. (BAE Systems Surface Ships South, late Vosper Thornycroft Shipbuilding)

E-BOATS SUNK IN DIRECT ACTION AGAINST SURFACE VESSELS:

S 38 sunk by destroyers HMS *Garth* and HMS *Campbell*, 20 November 1940

S 63 sunk by ramming by destroyer HMS *Mackay*, 25 October 1943

S 71 sunk by destroyers HMS *Garth* and HMS *Montrose*, 17 February 1943

S 119 sunk by British warships, 8 March 1943

S 136 sunk by frigate HMS *Duff*, the destroyer *HMCS Souix* and the Polish destroyer *Krakowiak*, 11 June 1944

S 141 sunk by French destroyer *La Combattante*, 13 May 1944

S 147 sunk by French destroyer *La Combattante*, 25 April 1944

S 183 sunk by frigate HMS *Stayner* and MTBs 724 and 728, 19 September 1944

S 185 sunk by frigates HMS *Torrington*, HMS *Curzon* and HMS *Kittiwake*, 23 December 1944

S 192 sunk by frigates HMS *Torrington*, HMS *Curzon* and HMS *Kittiwake*, 23 December 1944

S 200 sunk by frigate HMS *Stayner* and MTBs 724 and 728, 19 September 1944

S 220 sunk by frigate HMS *Seymour*, 1 March 1945

S 702 sunk by frigate HMS *Stayner* and MTBs 724 and 728, 19 September 1944

E-BOATS SUNK IN COMBAT WITH COASTAL CRAFT:

S 29 sunk by MGB 333, 29 March 1943

S 77 sunk by MGBs 40 and 42, 25 July 1943

S 88 sunk by MTB 607, 25 October 1943

S 96 sunk in collision with ML 145, 25 September 1943

S 111 sunk after capture by MGBs 87, 88 and 91, 15 March 1942

S 176 sunk by MTBs 493, 494 and 497, 7 April 1945

S 177 sunk by MTBs 493, 494 and 497, 7 April 1945

S 182 sunk in collision with MTB 412, 27 July 1944

CONCLUSION

Post-war development of warships saw a move away from battleships and battlecruisers, these types having shown their vulnerability to both air and submarine attack. Quite apart from its vulnerability, and sheer cost, the battleship simply was no longer needed. The day of the smaller warship had arrived. On the German side, the E-Boats had scored the highest total of enemy shipping sunk after the U-Boats. Given the relatively low production cost of E-Boats compared with larger surface warships, they had certainly proven themselves as cost-effective weapons. Of the truly large warships, only the aircraft carrier would continue through into the 21st century. As the weaponry carried on warships became ever more sophisticated, and particularly with the advent of anti-ship missiles, smaller vessels would eventually have the kind of destructive firepower formerly carried by heavy cruisers and even battleships.

The current German *Albatros*-class *Schnellboot* is some 58m in length and displaces 398 tonnes. It has a top speed of 40 knots and is armed with two 76mm cannon and four Exocet missiles, as well as a sophisticated radar and communications system. Torpedo tubes are no longer carried.

Although the Royal Navy no longer operates any vessels that could be considered equivalent to the MTBs of World War II, the Vosper firm that manufactured so many of the vessels continued after the war to produce fast, powerful patrol boats for export, such as the 30m-long *Brave*-class, capable of speeds up to 52 knots and armed with four 533mm torpedo tubes and a 40mm Bofors gun.

In both cases the lineage is clear, the German vessels being larger and more powerfully armed and the British-designed vessels depending on speed and agility. Both German and British wartime types heavily influenced post-war thinking, and promoted the development of very fast coastal vessels capable of delivering a powerful blow against ships much larger than themselves.

A total of 239 E-Boats served with the German Navy from the launch of S 1 through to the end of the war, and of these some 99 survived. The majority were taken as prizes by the US, British and Soviet navies, with some later finding their way into the navies of Norway and Denmark. Two (S 130 and S 208) were even returned to Germany to serve as training vessels in the new Bundesmarine. E-Boat losses were nowhere near as catastrophic as those of the U-Boats, with around 767 crew members either KIA or MIA from a total of 7,500, representing a casualty rate of just over 10 per cent as opposed to more than 80 per cent for U-Boats.

Again, like their underwater counterparts, during the latter part of the war the E-Boats suffered badly from air attack; although fast-moving, the E-Boat did not offer a particularly stable gun platform for anti-aircraft weaponry, but its relatively large size presented a good target for enemy aircraft. Some 14 E-Boats were sunk by direct air attack (as distinct from being destroyed during general bombing raids on their bases). Most E-Boat operations, in fact, took place at night under cover of darkness.

During the course of World War II, E-Boats were responsible for the sinking of 101 Allied merchant ships representing more than 214,000 tonnes. A further 37 ships totalling over 148,000 tons were sunk by mines laid by E-Boats. These craft were also responsible for sinking 13 destroyers, 13 minesweepers, 12 LSTs, a minelayer and a submarine, as well as a number of smaller craft, including MTBs, by direct attack and by mines.

The men who served in the E-Boats were accorded considerable respect by their British adversaries, and in fact when Korvettenkapitän Kurt Fimmen and Kapitänleutnant Rebensburg sailed into Felixstowe with Konteradmiral Breuning on 13 May 1945 to surrender, they were treated to an honours salute.

During World War II, British MTBs and MGBs fought in several theatres of war. Those in the waters around the British coast were involved in at least 460 engagements with the enemy. During these actions some 269 enemy ships were sunk, with a loss to British forces of around 76 of their own vessels. The British crews of these small coastal craft were also highly respected by their German counterparts. At least one German flotilla commander, on seeing a British MTB return to rescue stricken fellow sailors whose boat was sinking, addressed his men and told them that he hoped that if they found themselves in a similar situation, they would behave in the same way as their British counterparts had done.

Vosper's boat-building expertise was also sought by foreign customers. Sweden ordered four 60ft boats, but only two – T.3, seen here, and T.4 – were delivered before wartime demands ensured that subsequent production was retained for the use of the Royal Navy. (BAE Systems Surface Ships South, late Vosper Thornycroft Shipbuilding)

BIBLIOGRAPHY

Beaver, Paul, *E-Boats and Coastal Craft*, Patrick Stevens Limited, Cambridge (1980)

Connolly, T. Garth, *Vosper MTBs in Action*, Squadron/Signal Publications, Texas (2000)

Connolly, T. Garth and Krakow, David L., *Schnellboot in Action*, Squadron/Signal Publications, Texas (2003)

Cooper, Bryan, *The War of the Gunboats*, Pen & Sword, Barnsley (2009)

Dallies-Labourdette, Jean-Philippe, *S-Boot – German E-Boats in Action 1939–45*, Histoire & Collections, Paris (2003)

Fock, Harald, *Die deutschen Schnellboote 1914–45*, Koehler Verlag, Hamburg (2001)

Frank, Hans, *E-Boats in Action in the Second World War*, Seaforth Publishing, Barnsley (2007)

Jackson, Robert, *Kriegsmarine*, Aurum Press, London (2001)

Jefferson, David, *Coastal Forces at War*, Haynes Publishing, Sparkford (1996)

Konstam, Angus, *British Motor Torpedo Boat 1939–45*, Osprey Publishing, Oxford (2003)

Kuhn, Vollmar, *Schnellboote im Einsatz*, Motorbuch Verlag, Stuttgart (1976)

Whitley, M.J., *German Coastal Forces of World War Two*, Arms & Armour Press, London (1992)

Williamson, Gordon, *German E-Boats 1939–45*, Osprey Publishing, Oxford (2002)

INDEX